Baking Magic

"Sasha brings a unique spin to classic desserts and shares some of her mouthwatering Ukrainian family recipes that you'll quickly adopt as your own. This is a cookbook that you'll reach for time and again for special occasions or a simple treat for the family."

—Stefani Pollack, founder of Cupcake Project

"Sasha Nary creates beautiful, show-stopping desserts. Sasha is brilliant; she shares her gorgeous and approachable designs that elevate desserts beyond your own imagination. She introduces us to her Ukrainian family's special signature dessert recipes and I'm here for it!"

—Emily Hutchinson, founder of The Hutch Oven,
best-selling cookbook author and TV personality

"Sasha is a phenomenal cake artist and a true dessert visionary. Her techniques are simple to follow and the results are consistently superb, even for beginner bakers. If you're looking to up your baking game, BUY THIS BOOK! Then follow her online and get to know the uber talented, oh so sweet Sasha Nary. I guarantee you'll love her as much as I and hundreds of thousands of others do."

—Elise Strachan, founder of My Cupcake Addiction

"Sasha puts a new twist on delicious classics, celebrating a modern approach to baking and sharing edible joy!"

—Katherine Sabbath, author, baker, business owner

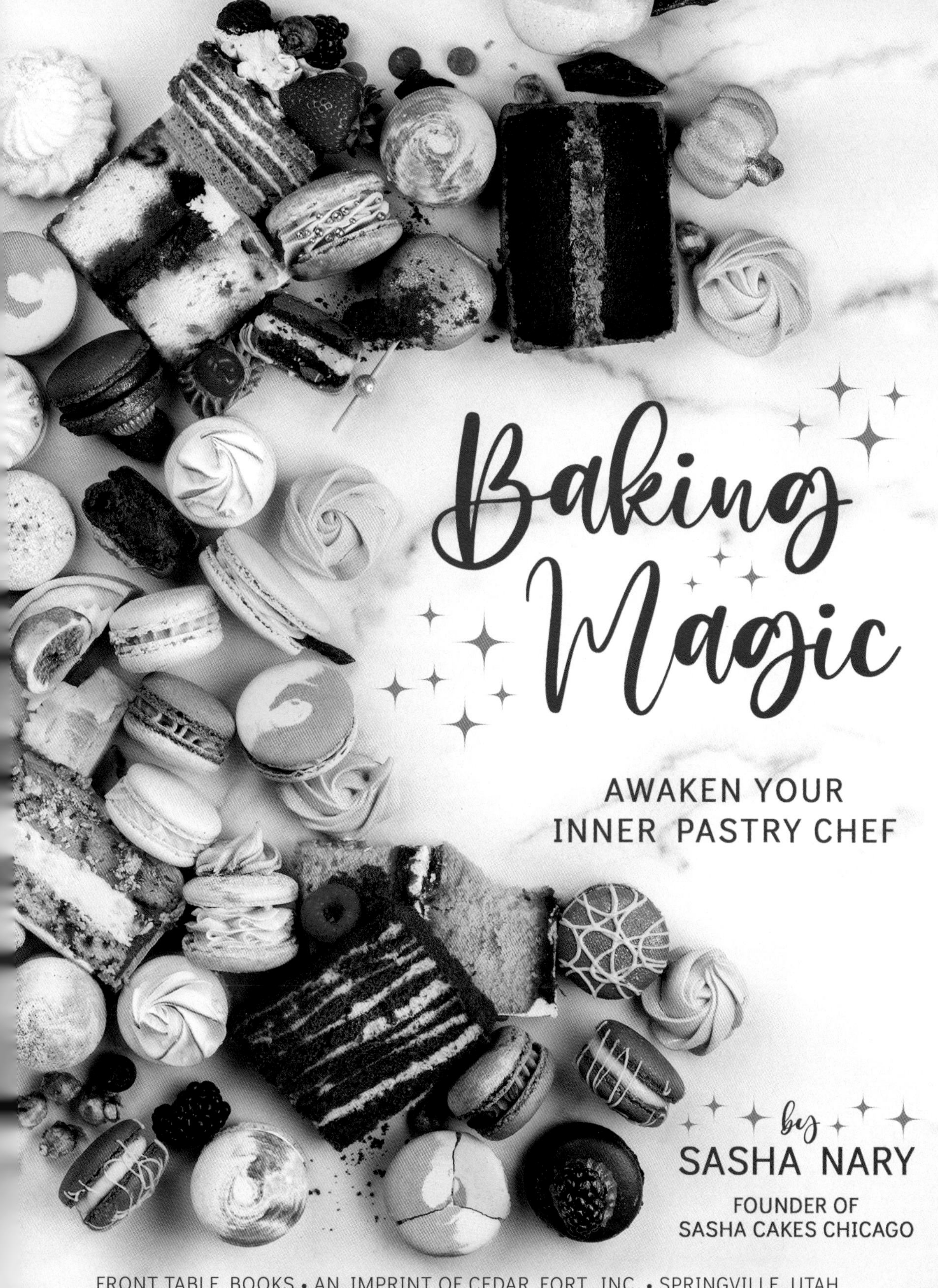

Baking Magic

AWAKEN YOUR INNER PASTRY CHEF

by
SASHA NARY
FOUNDER OF
SASHA CAKES CHICAGO

FRONT TABLE BOOKS • AN IMPRINT OF CEDAR FORT, INC. • SPRINGVILLE, UTAH

ISBN 13: 978-1-4621-4287-3

Published by Front Table Books, an imprint of Cedar Fort, Inc.
2373 W. 700 S., Springville, UT 84663
Distributed by Cedar Fort, Inc., www.cedarfort.com

Library of Congress Control Number: 2022937528

Cover design and interior layout and design by Shawnda T. Craig
Cover design © 2022 Cedar Fort, Inc.
Edited by Rachel Hathcock
Typeset by Shawnda T. Craig

Printed in the United States of America

10 9 8 7 6 5 4 3 2 1

Printed on acid-free paper

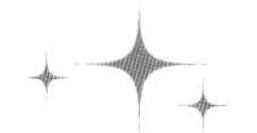

ACKNOWLEDGMENTS

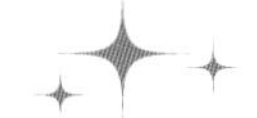

To my loves—my husband and our three treasures—our kids: I love you enormously and thank you from the bottom of my heart for always supporting me, for always being by my side: from endless taste tests to honest and best opinions, to recommendations and ideas, to numerous ingredient runs, dish washing and fixes, patience and giving me space when any baking disaster happens. You are my everything and I am so lucky to call myself your wife and your mom.

To hubby: there wouldn't be me without you. Ever. I love you more than cake.

To Alan, my oldest: your eye for flavor combinations and tastes are stellar. You are a big part of who I am now, and I'll always cherish that.

To Aiden, my middle son: you inspire me every day. The artist in you made me a cake artist today. Your ideas and creativity are in everything I create.

To Arielle, our youngest: you made me pursue my dream. The princess in you woke up a baking queen in me.

To Mom: you and Grandma made this baker and recipe developer. Thank you for all your love, care, baking and life lessons.

To Dad: I know you would have been very proud of me now and would have loved eating those Rose Meringue Cookies with your mom's homemade cocoa.

To my family, friends, followers, clients, and students: thank you for always being there for me, believing in me, and always supporting my dreams and my business.

To the team at Cedar Fort Publishing: thank you from the bottom of my heart for the opportunity to work on this amazing project and allowing me to share my love and passion of baking in this breathtaking book.

Love, Sasha

CONTENTS

Chapter 6

Information

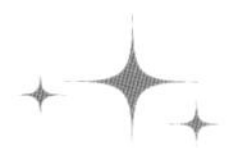

A NOTE FROM SASHA

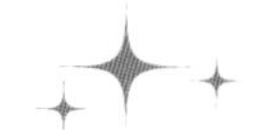

The recipes, tips, tricks, and my ultimate secrets that I am sharing here are for bakers of any level and type of experience: from a novice or hobby baker to experienced pastry chefs and professionals. Some of the recipes are my family's treasures, signatures that I have translated from our language, improved, and adapted to US ingredients. Plus, my own, highly cherished, and coveted recipes that were developed, tested, and held onto for years. I am giving it all to you, with all my heart full of love of desserts, decorating, designing, and inspiring others. This book is my "Magic of Baking", that will awaken the pastry chef in you. Every recipe and every photo, from classic to inventive, has my own personal flair and touch.

From Ukrainian nostalgia and my families' signature desserts that will leave you drooling after just reading the ingredients list (including eggless), to my go-to long awaited "tested, tried, and tested again" best cake recipes including Sugar-Free options, and the magical pastries, plus my ultimate passion: macarons, pavlova's and meringue treats, and mini tarts. In this book I am also sharing my two inventions: the Reuse/Reduce Macaron Recipe, plus the ultimate "earthquake" in the baking world as we know it: The Eggless Heat and Humidity Resistant Buttercream.

Dive in, have a lot of fun, experiment, practice, celebrate even the smallest wins, and don't forget to share with me your delicious creations by tagging @sashacakeschicago and #BakingMagicBook.

INTRODUCTION

I dream of desserts

Every other night I wake up with a new recipe idea, decorating vision, or construction of a dessert. That is why there is a notebook on my nightstand.

When it comes to sharing what baking, dough, batter, and frosting mean to me—I could never quite clearly explain that, until the time when I started writing this book. Why is that you ask? It's not just that a "party without a cake is just a meeting" as Julia Child said, it's more than that. Some connections/memories of baking are bittersweet, such as my sweet grandma Lyuda who whipped up the most fairy-like sweets and treats in her tiny kitchen of Sevastopol, Soviet Union's apartment building. I remember the windows open, the Black Sea breeze and cherry tree aromas, mixing with her magical slowly bubbling rose jam and strawberry coulis on the stove, while meringue cookies are baking in the oven. I baked my first cake and cookies alongside my grandma when I was 8 years old. Just like all my family members: I am obsessed with sweets, desserts, cakes, chocolate, and ice-cream. True story: when I was about 12 years old, I announced that from now on I am on a chocolate diet, and I committed to eat exclusively chocolate for 2 weeks Obviously, I lasted only a day or so, but my mom and sister still talk about "that amazing diet of mine." We have baked a lot together with my grandma and I was so fascinated of how skillfully she breaded the dough for her pies, how she piped the tiny roses and leaves with a paper piping bag (no tips) on the Kiev Cake. She passed away when I was 11, and baking with her, playing with seashells on the beach, and reading together are the most vivid dreams of my childhood.

Fast forward 3 years or so and you'll find me in the kitchen again, baking with my mom—who due to lack of money, nationwide poverty following the crash of USSR and the loss of her job has become extremely creative with previously canned fruits, vegetables, and ginormous bags of sugar and flour (which is all we had left at some point). Mom whipped up the most creative sweet and savory pies to brighten up our days and satisfy our sweet tooth—from braiding the prettiest canned apple and cherry pies, to vegan cookies, to made from scratch pizza's.

While the middle, high, and music schools, university, and an overwhelming move from Ukraine to USA didn't leave me much time to bake as often as I desired—I caught up later in my life. As things settled (and started) in the USA—from acclimatization, to learning a completely new language, studying at night in yet another, now USA University, meeting the love of my life and now husband. Then planning a wedding/getting married, finally getting our rainbow pregnancy (walking down the stage for my diploma in heels and 8 months pregnant). Not long after having our second son and all while always needing and wanting to work—my only creative outlets for 17 years were makeup artistry and the skincare field. This industry gave me freedom of expression, career growth and opportunity to inspire, teach, and manage others. It also helped many people become happy and educated about skincare, makeup, and self-care. And then a miracle happened: as we had our third and long-awaited daughter, life gears shifted completely. While on semi-bed rest, and on maternity leave later, I started baking more and more from baking for special family gatherings only, to every day. My main goal was to master all the French desserts that I had the pleasure of devouring while visiting Paris a few years back. And so, it started. It will never end. I found my way of "experimenting and creating", that girl that got all A's and took the 1st place in all Chemistry classes and even National competitions back in Ukraine, that girl that only wanted to eat chocolate for 2 weeks, that girl that learned so much from her grandma and mom about the science of baking, while melting in happiness seeing others devour her bakes—finally found herself. But I didn't do it on my own. That path of finding "me" was accompanied in partnership with incredible husband, kids, family, friends, and relatives' support. From a dear friend and client of mine who pushed me to start posting my bakes on social media and made me believe in myself and referred me to every single person she has ever come across to, to the most important, my one and only—my husband. He saw "it" before I did. He ran home one day after work, cheerfully handing my first cake turntable, piping bags, and collection of piping tips and said: "Go for it! You never know where it will take you." He supports my every move, my every crazy idea. As unbelievable as it sounds (even to me)—he went all in with my decision to leave a career of an Account Executive for a major fashion and cosmetic company, to starting my own business as a baker, content creator, and recipe developer. Don't even get me started on who is first to try all my new recipes and how much he has to try.

And here I am, 4 years have passed since I've made this life-changing career decision. I've gone from learning how to make macarons to clients all over the USA that get my desserts shipped to them from across the nation. Then to numerous partnerships and collaborations with world renowned brands and companies, to teaching online baking and decorating courses, creating my own line of baking supplies, to being a contestant on Food Network and numerous features on local TV channels. I am here to simply inspire you by sharing my story. I want to inspire you to jump forward in pursuit of your dreams and desires (even if they're not baking related), or most importantly—inspire or wake up a Baking Magician in you. Yes, you. If you ever think: "I cannot do that, I'll fail." I ask you to please grab this book and read this page again. If I could do it, after barely baking for 20 years while immigrating, studying, surviving, then building a family—then you can also. We all have our own natural clock, and nothing is ever too late, nothing is ever impossible. So, let's make it magical, let's bake, and let's create.

CHAPTER 1

Baking 101

Before you jump into actual recipes, I would love to share the Essential Supplies and Equipment list that I personally started and continue working with.

SUPPLIES & TOOLS

Besides the standard baking supplies such as measuring spoons, bowls and whisks, here are some things that will make your baking and decorating process easier. They are essential to have for the execution of the recipes in this book.

- Stand and Hand Mixers
- Digital Kitchen Scale
- Candy Thermometer
- Oven Thermometer
- Three 6 x 3-inch round cake pans
- Two 8 x 3-inch round cake pans
- Wilton Easy Layers Set 8-inch
- Wilton Easy Layers Set 6-inch
- Bundt Baking Pan
- Baking Non-Stick Spray (I prefer Wilton's Bake Easy Spray)
- Baking Strips *see note below
- Cake Decorating Turntable
- Cake Rounds/Drums/Boards
- Offset and Silicone Spatulas
- Small and Large Cake Scrapers
- Piping Bags
- Piping Tips (by Wilton: 1A, 2A,1M, 1D, 8B, 134, 34)
- Rolling Pin
- Parchment (Silicone Free) Paper
- Cling Film/Kitchen Plastic/Glade
- Silicone Baking Mats (preferred)
- Mini Tart Mesh Rings (or any mini tart baking molds/pans)
- Cookie Cutters
- Cake Leveler or Serrated Knife
- 12 Cavity Cupcake Baking Pan
- Cupcake Tins
- Heatproof Bowls
- Mesh Sifter

- Drip Bottle (for chocolate ganache drips)
- Striped Combs, such as a Bengal Comb by Ester Cakes
- Optional: edible luster or metallic dusts, edible gold leaf, sparkling sugars, sprinkles
- Optional: Wilton Christmas Tree Baking Pans
- Optional: printed large heart and Christmas templates
- Measuring/Weighing Ingredients

I cannot stress enough how important it is to use a Digital Kitchen Scale to measure your ingredients. My favorite one is from good old Amazon—it has worked perfectly for 10 years already and was inexpensive. It is not accurate to measure your ingredients in volume/cups, especially when you are scooping the measuring cup with dry ingredients. A small change of volume will tremendously alter the recipe with the worst possible results. All the recipes in this book are in grams, for maximum precision.

BAKING TEMPERATURES

Using a separate oven thermometer will open your eyes. All ovens are different, and sometimes even the age of the oven affects its temperature's performance. Hang your separate oven thermometer on the middle rack and compare its readings to the actual oven's thermometer/display. Almost always you will see a discrepancy, sometimes a tremendous one. Go with a separate, in-oven thermometer. This is especially important when it comes to baking macarons.

Always bake your cakes on the middle rack and use only as many cake pans as can fit on that rack at one time. Blocking the oven's heat on the top or bottom racks will result in improperly baked, raised cake, possible browning/burning, and even unbaked/soggy centers.

You will learn in all my cake recipes that I recommend using the "low and slow" oven baking method. This means baking pretty much anything at lower temperatures for a longer time. The result: evenly raised beautifully baked cakes, cupcakes, and cookies. Plus, you have the assurance of keeping the colored baked goods from browning

COOLING AND LEVELING/TORTE OF BAKED CAKE LAYERS

My main advice when it comes to baked cake layers is to never try leveling or cutting it (torte) when it's at room temperature: you will end up with a crumbled, uneven, broken mess. Always flip the cakes upside down on a wire rack with the baking pan still intact. This will promote flat tops if yours didn't bake as such to begin with. Once the cake/baking pan has cooled off to room temperature, remove the pan and wrap the cake layer with one or two layers of kitchen plastic/cling film/Glad. Place into the refrigerator or freezer for at least a few hours, but I highly recommend leaving them there overnight. You may place a cake round in between each wrapped plastic cake layer to prevent them pushing down on each other. Working with cold cake layers is 100% easier than when they are at room temperature.

INGREDIENT TEMPERATURES

Always use room temperature ingredients, unless mentioned otherwise in the recipe. Room temperature ingredients emulsify and combine with each other better then cold. Remember: your sugar, flour, salt, and cocoa are at room temperature, always and forever. When you add cold eggs, butter, or milk—what kind of reaction will take place? It will curdle, which will result in dense, dry, hard cakes. The best way to prepare your ingredients is to simply remove your normally cold ingredients from the refrigerator and keep them at room temperature for at least an hour before starting to work on any cake recipe. What if you forgot to do that? Here are my tricks:

Eggs: place in the bowl with warm water for 5–10 minutes.

Milk: microwave or heat on stove's lowest heat for 30 seconds.

Butter: pour hot water into a bowl. Then pour the water out and cover your sticks of butter with that warm bowl for a few minutes. Voila—room temperature butter.

Sour cream: measure out needed weight of sour cream and place that cup/bowl in another bowl with warm water.

HOW TO/DIY

Caster and Powdered Sugar: make your own by pulsing a granulated sugar in your blender/food processor. A few pulses will give you super fine or caster sugar. If you pulse longer, you will get powdered sugar.

Freeze-Dried Fruit Powder: simply pulse in your blender or food processor.

Baking Strips: if you've seen my viral Instagram video—I make my own and highly recommend for you to do the same. That is unless you already have or prefer to buy the baking strips (Wilton is one of the brands that sells them). Simply cut out strips from any fabric: old sheets, kitchen towels, tea towels (or any old and washed fabric) long enough to tie around your baking pans.

Baking Spray: if you are not using the Bake Easy Spray by Wilton or any other nonstick cooking spray—here is how to prep your pans without it: grease the bottom and sides of pans with butter and then lightly dust with flour. Alternatively, you may use parchment paper rounds on the bottom of your pans.

Now that you have "graduated" my Baking 101 class, it is time to dive into the Recipes.

CHAPTER 2

Buttercream Basics

7 DELICIOUS, EASY-TO-MAKE BUTTERCREAM RECIPES, INCLUDING THE SUGAR-FREE, EGGLESS, AND MY NEW INVENTION, THE HEAT AND HUMIDITY RESISTANT BUTTERCREAM

EGGLESS CONDENSED MILK BUTTERCREAM—A FAMILY CLASSIC

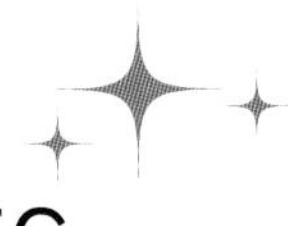

I am starting this chapter with the famous, loved, and mega easy to make Condensed Milk Buttercream. How can I not love everything about it if I was probably born with it in my feeding bottle? This Buttercream, simply made with butter and condensed milk, is a signature frosting in Eastern Europe and former Soviet Union countries. Almost every single dessert that I've ever eaten while growing up in Ukraine was made with this delicious frosting: from pastries, cookies, to simple and intricate cakes. To be honest, I understand why. It is light, silky, fluffy, incredibly delicious, and pipes beautifully. But most importantly for any home, hobby, or even savvy baker—it is easy to make, and it develops color beautifully—requiring less food coloring then most of the buttercreams. You've got to know a few tips and tricks, and that's what I'll help you with today.

To make this Buttercream you just need butter and sweetened condensed milk, adding salt and vanilla (or other flavorings) is optional. In my recipe below I skipped salt and vanilla since I love the taste of condensed milk. Because it is not too sweet or overwhelming there is no need to add anything else, but this can be a personal preference.

CONDENSED MILK BUTTERCREAM USES

The possibilities for using this Buttercream are endless: from filling and decorating your sponge/chiffon cakes, to beautifully piped cupcakes, macarons, and many other desserts. It also takes color beautifully—my suggestion is to always use gel food colorings.

STORING CONDENSED MILK BUTTERCREAM

I highly recommend using Condensed Milk Buttercream within just a few hours of making it. Since it's so easy to make, there is no need to whip up large amounts. However, if you do have leftovers or had to make it in advance, store your freshly whipped Buttercream in airtight containers. You can refrigerate it for up to 7 days or freeze it for up to 30 days. Before rewhipping your refrigerated or frozen Buttercream let it come to room temperature.

INGREDIENTS:

226 g (1 cup, 2 sticks) unsalted butter, at room temperature

397 g (1 can) sweetened condensed milk, at room temperature

1 tsp. vanilla extract or emulsion, optional

Pinch of salt, optional

Directions:

1. In the bowl of a mixer fitted with a whisk attachment, whip the butter for approximately 8 minutes or until it has tripled in volume and becomes light and fluffy. Stop to scrape the bottom of the bowl a few times.
2. Add 1 teaspoon of vanilla extract or emulsion and the salt to the whipped butter. Now add 14 oz. sweetened condensed milk in thirds, whipping for about 8–10 seconds after each addition. Don't forget to scrape the bottom of the bowl after each addition.

TROUBLESHOOTING THAT IS APPLICABLE TO ANY OTHER BUTTERCREAM RECIPES

What may go wrong while making Condensed Milk Buttercream? Truly not much, if you carefully follow this recipe. Bring your sticks of butter to room temperature for an hour before making this buttercream. Whip it on high speed for no less than 8 minutes, and add your room temperature condensed milk carefully, in small portions while mixing on medium speed. These are the most important tricks. If your butter was too soft prior to adding the condensed milk, you may see your buttercream starting to separate. Don't panic, simply pop your mixer bowl with separated buttercream into the refrigerator for 10 minutes and then rewhip again. If your workspace is cold, Condensed Milk Buttercream may not whip up light and fluffy. In that case, just place half of it into a microwave safe bowl, warm up for 5–10 seconds, and rewhip with the other half.

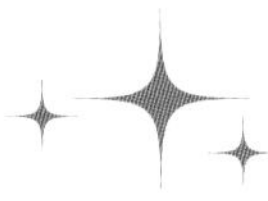

DULCE DE LECHE BUTTERCREAM

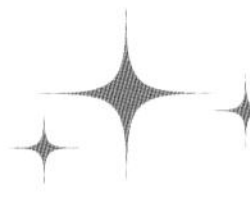

INGREDIENTS:

226 g (1 cup, 2 sticks) unsalted butter, at room temperature

397 g (1 can) homemade Dulce de Leche, at room temperature

Directions:

1. In the bowl of a mixer fitted with a whisk attachment, whip the butter for approximately 8 minutes or until it has tripled in volume and become light and fluffy. Stop to scrape the bottom of the bowl a few times.

2. Reduce the speed of the mixer to the lowest setting and add the previously prepared and cooled homemade Dulce de Leche in thirds, whipping for about 8–10 seconds after each addition. Don't forget to scrape the bottom of the bowl after each addition.

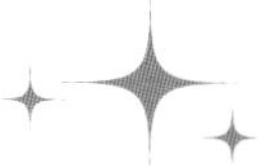

SUGAR-FREE SILKY BUTTERCREAM

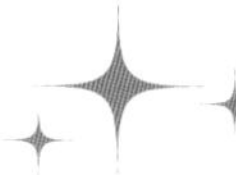

INGREDIENTS:

300 g (from 9 eggs) fresh or carton egg whites

150 g (3/4 cup) monk sugar

1/4 tsp. salt

565 g (2 1/2 cups, 5 sticks) room temperature/soft unsalted butter (leave out of fridge overnight)

1 tsp. pure vanilla extract

Directions:

1. Prepare a double boiler. Use a pot slightly larger in diameter than your mixing bowl. Fill it with a bit of water and place on medium-high heat.
2. Wipe your mixing bowl and whisk attachment with a bit of lemon juice or vinegar on a piece of paper towel. Place your egg whites, monk sugar, and salt into your mixer bowl and place the bowl into the pot with boiling water. Make sure that your mixer bowl with the egg whites and sugar does not touch the boiling water. Reduce the heat to medium-low to ensure that the water is barely simmering.
3. Whip your egg whites/sugar mixture with your whisk nonstop for approximately 3 minutes or until your sugar thermometer reaches 140 degrees/60 degrees. I use the whisk mixer attachment—fewer steps, fewer dishes to wash. Then check the mixture with your fingers—you should not be feeling any grains of sugar.
4. Transfer your mixing bowl to a stand mixer and start mixing on low speed. Gradually increase the speed to the highest setting. Mix it for 8 minutes until you get stiff peaks, meaning—when 8 minutes have passed, pull your whisk out and check the meringue's peak—it should just slightly curve.
5. Decrease mixer speed to medium and slowly add your 565 grams of unsalted butter, 1 tablespoon at a time. Then add 1 teaspoon of pure vanilla extract and mix on high speed for 4 minutes. At some point you might be seeing that your buttercream is looking soupy-do not panic. As you continue adding butter while mixing, the consistency will change.

MIND-BLOWING EASY EGGLESS CHOCOLATE BUTTERCREAM FROSTING

INGREDIENTS:

397 g (1 can) sweetened condensed milk, at room temperature

375 g (1 2/3 cup) unsalted butter, at room temperature

3–5 Tbsp. unsweetened cocoa powder

Directions:

1. Add all ingredients to the mixer bowl, fitted with a whisk attachment, and mix on high speed for approximately 5 minutes or until it doubles in volume, becomes fluffy and silky.

SIGNATURE TRADEMARK: HEAT AND HUMIDITY RESISTANT EGGLESS BUTTERCREAM

INGREDIENTS:

448 g white chocolate morsels (2 ½ cups), chips, or bar

230 g (1 cup) full fat sour cream

339 g (1 ½ cups, 3 sticks) unsalted butter, at room temperature

1 tsp. gelatin or agar powder (if preferred)

1 Tbsp. cold water

pinch of salt

clear vanilla or any other clear extract

Directions:

1. Place gelatin (or agar) powder and cold water into a small bowl, mix and set aside to bloom for 5 minutes.
2. Place white chocolate, salt, vanilla, and sour cream into a mixer bowl and over the double boiler, continuously mixing with a silicone spatula. Keep heating until all the chocolate melts.
3. Meanwhile, place butter into your mixer bowl fitted with the whisk attachment and whip the butter for at least 5 minutes or until it doubles in volume, becoming lighter and fluffy.
4. Take the chocolate/sour cream mixture from the double boiler.
5. Melt bloomed gelatin in microwave for 5–10 seconds and mix it into the sour cream/ chocolate mixture.
6. Stop the mixer and add the chocolate/sour cream mixture into the whipped butter.
7. Allow the buttercream to mix on low speed for about 1–2 minutes.
8. Remove the bowl from the mixer, cover it with kitchen plastic and place into freezer for 15 minutes or refrigerator for 30 minutes.
9. Once the buttercream has cooled off/ stabilized—place it back into the stand mixer and whisk again on medium speed for a few minutes, then on high speed for an additional 4 minutes.
10. To remove any excess air/bubbles beat the buttercream with a silicone spatula by hand or whip in mixer fitted with pedal attachment on low speed for a few minutes.

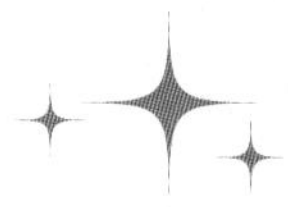

SIGNATURE SWISS MERINGUE BUTTERCREAM

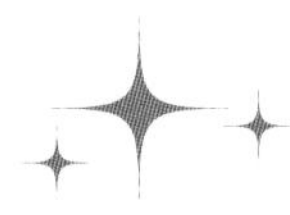

INGREDIENTS:

300 g (from 9 eggs) fresh or carton egg whites

250 g (1.1 cups) caster or superfine sugar

¼ tsp. salt

565 g (2.5 cups or 5 sticks) unsalted butter, at room temperature 1 tsp. pure vanilla extract

---

Directions:

1. Prepare a double boiler. Use a pot slightly larger in diameter than your mixing bowl. Fill it with a bit of water and place it on medium-high heat.
2. Wipe your mixing bowl and whisk attachment with lemon juice or vinegar on a piece of paper towel. Place your egg whites, caster sugar and salt into your mixing bowl and place the mixing bowl into the pot with boiling water. Make sure that your mixing bowl with egg whites and sugar does not touch the boiling water. Reduce the heat to medium-low to ensure that the water is barely simmering.
3. Whisk your egg whites/sugar mixture with your whisk nonstop for approximately 3 minutes or until your sugar thermometer reaches 140 degrees Fahrenheit/60 degrees Celsius. I use the whisk mixer attachment—fewer steps, fewer dishes to wash. Check mixture with your fingers—you should not be feeling any grains of sugar.
4. Transfer your mixing bowl to the stand mixer and start mixing on low speed, gradually increasing the speed to high. Mix on high for 8 minutes until you have stiff peaks. Meaning when 8 minutes have passed, pull your whisk out and check the meringue's peak—it should just slightly curve.
5. Decrease mixer speed to medium and slowly add your 565 grams of unsalted butter, 1 tablespoon at a time. Then add 1 teaspoon of pure vanilla extract and mix on high speed for 4 minutes. At some point you might be seeing that your buttercream is looking soupy—do not panic. As you continue adding butter while mixing, consistency will change.
6. Once 4 minutes have passed, decrease mixer speed to low and continue mixing for 2–4 minutes or longer, when possible, otherwise your Swiss Meringue Buttercream will have a lot of bubbles.

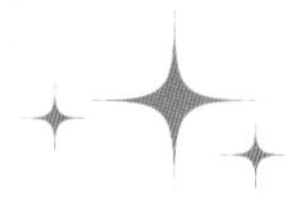

SIGNATURE FRENCH SILK BUTTERCREAM

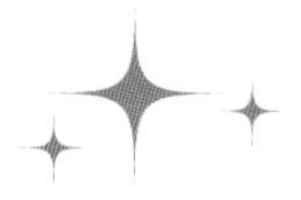

INGREDIENTS:

100 g (½ cup) granulated sugar

33 g (2 ¼ Tbsp.) water

5 large egg yolks

227 g (1 cup, 2 sticks) unsalted butter, at room temperature

1 tsp. pure vanilla extract

pinch of salt

Directions:

1. Combine sugar and water in a medium saucepan. Stir to combine and heat over low heat until sugar dissolves. Increase heat to medium-high and bring it to a boil.
2. Put the egg yolks in a stand mixer fitted with a whisk attachment and beat until thick and foamy, about 5 minutes.
3. Cook the sugar and water syrup until it reaches 240 degrees Fahrenheit on sugar thermometer. Immediately remove from the heat. With mixer still running, slowly drizzle hot syrup into a bowl with yolks, making sure that the sugar syrup is pouring directly on the egg yolks between the whisk attachment and the side of the bowl. Make sure not to get any sugar syrup onto the whisk attachment.
4. Continue mixing on high speed for approximately 5 minutes or until the bottom of the bowl is cool to the touch and the yolk mixture has cooled to room temperature.
5. Once the egg yolk/sugar syrup mixture has cooled, reduce the mixer speed to the lowest speed and add in butter one tablespoon at a time, allowing each piece to incorporate before adding the next. Add vanilla and salt. Continue mixing until buttercream is smooth and creamy, for about 5-6 minutes.

CHAPTER 3

From Ukraine with love

14 OF MY SIGNATURE FAMILY RECIPES REVAMPED AND MODERNIZED BY ME, ADAPTED TO MODERN INGREDIENTS, INCLUDING THE USE OF USA AND INTERNATIONAL QUALITY OF SUPPLIES AND COMPONENTS.

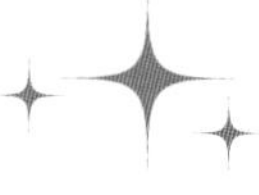

BEST KEPT FAMILY SECRET: THE ULTIMATE CHOCOLATIEST CAKE

THIS CAKE IS EVERYTHING! Chocolatiest indulgence at its best. You will not believe how easy it is to make it and how incredibly delicious it is until you try this recipe. This cake has been an ultimate staple in my family for three generations: every holiday, every birthday, requested by family, friends, neighbors year after year. I have never shared this recipe, cherishing and holding onto it for a moment as this one and now it proudly opens up my first book. Enormous thanks to my sister who kept the original recipe, handwritten by my grandmother, and gave it to me when I started baking full time few years ago. *PRO TIP: For Gluten Free version of this recipe, simply substitute the all-purpose flour with 1:1 Gluten Free flour.

CHOCOLATE CAKE:

300 g (1 ½ cups + 2 Tbsp.) granulated sugar

3 eggs, at room temperature

305 g (1 cup) sweetened condensed milk, at room temperature

3–5 Tbsp. unsweetened cocoa powder

360 g (1 ½ cups) sour cream, at room temperature

270 g (2 ⅛ cups) all-purpose flour

1 tsp. pure vanilla extract

½ tsp. baking soda

CHOCOLATE CREAM:

1 can (397 g) sweetened condensed milk, at room temperature

395 g (1 ¾ cups, 3 ½ sticks) unsalted butter, at room temperature

5 Tbsp. unsweetened cocoa powder

GARNISH:

Grated chocolate bar/chocolate shavings and finely chopped walnuts (optional)

Chocolate Cake Directions:

1. Preheat oven to 320 degrees Fahrenheit.
2. Sift together flour and baking soda and set aside
3. Add eggs and sugar to the bowl of a stand mixer, fitted with a whisk attachment, and mix on high speed for approximately 5 minutes or until the mixture becomes fluffy and lighter in color.
4. Reduce the mixer speed to low (stir) and add condensed milk, cocoa powder, sour cream, and vanilla while the mixer is still whisking on the lowest speed.
5. Once all ingredients in the bowl are fully mixed in/incorporated, add pre-sifted soda and flour. Allow the dry ingredients to incorporate while mixer is on low speed, then gradually increase the speed to high and mix for approximately 5 minutes.
6. Fill two of the 8-inch x 3-inch greased cake baking pans with the batter and bake on the middle rack of your oven for 30-40 minutes. Bake until an inserted toothpick comes out clean, dry, and free of crumbles.
7. Once cakes are baked, flip them over/ upside down onto your cooling rack. Do not remove the baking pans until they cool to room temperature. Once the pans have cooled, remove the baked cake layers. Wrap each cake layer into a kitchen plastic/cling film and refrigerate for at least a few hours. Alternatively, you may freeze the plastic wrapped cake layers overnight or longer. Before filling and decorating the cakes, allow the frozen cakes to thaw in refrigerator for a few hours or overnight.
8. Level, if needed, and cut each cake layer in half horizontally once it has chilled in the refrigerator or freezer.

Chocolate Cream Directions:

1. Add all ingredients to the mixer bowl, fitted with a whisk attachment, and mix them on high speed until they double in volume and become fluffy and silky, approximately 5 minutes.

Assembly:

1. Once you have torted your cakes and cut each baked layer in half (resulting in 4 cake layers), it is time to fill and stack the cake.
2. Place your cake drum/board on a turntable and add a small amount of the chocolate cream to the center of the cake drum/round.
3. Place one cake layer over a smoothed small amount of cream, lightly press, and then spread approximately half a cup of the chocolate cream over the cake layer. Smooth and straighten it out with the offset spatula.
4. Repeat with the remaining cake layers and cream. Smooth and even out the sides of the cake with a bench or cake scraper.
5. Refrigerate the filled cake for at least 30 minutes or freeze for 15 minutes. Then finish decorating with grated chocolate and walnuts, if desired.
6. Cut, serve, and enjoy.

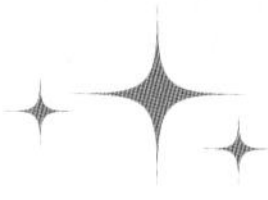

GRANDMA'S SIGNATURE HONEY CAKE (AUTHENTIC RECIPE)

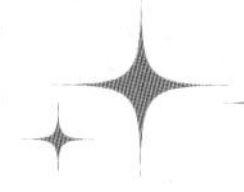

If you have ever dived into classic eastern European baking recipes, chances are you have heard of Medovik–The Honey Cake. It is known to be one of the more difficult ones to make, however I've never understood why. Maybe because I have such a fantastic recipe? These super thin, porous, honey cookie-like layers that absorb the delightful sour cream-based filling will not leave you dissatisfied–a true honey indulgence for a true honey lover. This is one of those desserts that taste the absolute best the next day, as the cake layers need time to absorb the filling. *PRO TIP: For Gluten Free version of this recipe, simply substitute the all-purpose flour with 1:1 Gluten Free flour.

HONEY CAKE LAYERS:

180 g (½ cup) honey

50 g granulated sugar

110 g (½ cup, one stick) unsalted butter

1 tsp. baking soda

4 large eggs, at room temperature

¼ tsp. salt

1 tsp. vanilla extract

450 g (3 5/8 cups) all-purpose flour

FILLING:

460 g (2 cups) sour cream

1 can (397 g) sweetened condensed milk

113 g (½ cup, one stick) unsalted butter, at room temperature

HONEY SWISS MERINGUE BUTTERCREAM:

300 g (from 9 eggs) fresh or carton egg whites, at room temperature225 g (1 cup) caster or superfine sugar

¼ tsp. salt

565 g (2 ½ cups, 5 sticks) unsalted butter, at room temperature 1 tsp. pure vanilla extract

4 Tbsp. honey

DECORATIONS:

White Chocolate Honeycomb Shards, Honey drip

Honey Cake Directions:

1. In a saucepan combine butter, honey and sugar and place on medium heat. Simmer for 3–4 minutes, until it changes color to a darker shade. Stir in the baking soda. Take off the heat and set aside for 2–3 mins. Beat eggs in a separate bowl with a hand whisk, and slowly drizzle the eggs into the hot butter/honey mixture, continuously whisking it the whole time. Whisk it until the eggs are completely incorporated.
2. Stir in the salt and vanilla. Fold in flour in portions of 3. This is going to be thick sticky dough.
3. Immediately pour out the dough onto a clean floured surface or onto a floured baking paper. Sprinkle flour over the dough. Lightly roll it into a thick tube just enough to be able to cut it into 14 equal parts. Dust with more flour as needed.
4. Place another parchment paper coordinating with your baking sheet in size onto your work surface, dust the parchment paper with flour. Place one dough ball on it, dust some flour over it and gently start rolling it to make a big cookie more than 8 inches in diameter. To trim it into a neat 6-inch cookie I used a 6-inch cake pan. You could use a 6-inch plate or anything of that approximate size. Save the trimmings and use them for rolling/cutting more cake layers. Poke the cookie with a fork to avoid bubble formations while baking.
5. Preheat oven to 380 degrees Fahrenheit. To make the handling easy and less time consuming, just slide in the parchment paper with the cutout cookie round onto a baking tray and bake for 6–7 minutes until it turns a nice golden-brown color. In the meantime, repeat the above steps with remaining dough.
6. After 6–7 mins in the oven, it should be a little firm and darker on the sides. Do not peel parchment paper off the honey cookie until it has completely cooled off on a cooling rack.

Honey Swiss Meringue Buttercream Directions:

1. Prepare a double boiler. I use a pot slightly larger in diameter than my mixing bowl. Fill it with a bit of water and place it on medium-high heat.
2. Wipe your mixing bowl and whisk attachment with lemon juice or vinegar on a piece of paper towel. Place your egg whites, caster sugar and salt into your mixing bowl and place the mixing bowl into a pot with boiling water. Make sure that your mixing bowl with egg whites and sugar does not touch the boiling water. Reduce the heat to medium-low to ensure that the water is barely simmering.
3. Whisk your egg whites/sugar mixture with your whisk nonstop for approximately 3 minutes or until your sugar thermometer reaches 140 degrees Fahrenheit/60 degrees Celsius. I use the whisk mixer attachment—fewer steps, fewer dishes to wash. Check mixture with your fingers—you should not be feeling any grains of sugar.

4. Transfer your mixing bowl to a stand mixer and start mixing on low speed, gradually increasing the speed to the highest. Mix on high for 8 minutes until you have stiff peaks, meaning when 8 minutes have passed, pull your whisk out and check the meringue's peak—it should just slightly curve.
5. Decrease the mixer speed to medium and slowly add your 565 grams of unsalted butter, 1 tablespoon at a time. Then add 1 teaspoon of pure vanilla extract, honey, and mix on high speed for 4 minutes.
6. Now, an important step—once 4 minutes have passed, decrease mixer speed to low speed and continue mixing for 2 minutes, otherwise your Swiss Meringue Buttercream will have a lot of bubbles.
7. Coloring your Swiss Meringue Buttercream: I love to use Roxy & Rich Fondusts, Wilton Color Right System Gels, as well as Americolor and Chefmaster Gels.

Assembly:

1. Once the cake/cookie layers have chilled, start building the cake by alternating honey cake layers with sour cream filling.
2. Place the stacked cake into the refrigerator for at least one hour or into a freezer for 30 minutes.
3. After the honey cake has chilled and settled, it is ready for frosting with honey Swiss meringue buttercream, honey drip, and chocolate decorations.

HONEY CUPCAKES
THE MINI HONEY CAKES (MINI MEDOVIK)

MAKES 10–12 CUPCAKES

Of course, I had to twist the classic. Don't we love everything mini? Your already favorite (or soon to be) Medovik (the honey cake) in a cupcake form. *PRO TIP: For Gluten Free version of this recipe, simply substitute the all-purpose flour with 1:1 Gluten Free flour.

HONEY CAKE:

85 g (4 Tbsp.) honey

1 tsp. baking soda

113 g ½ cup, 1 stick) unsalted butter, at room temperature

3 eggs, at room temperature

100 g (½ cup) granulated sugar

180 g (1 ½ cups) all-purpose flour

CREAM FILLING:

180 g (¾ cups) heavy cream, cold

85 g (¾ cup) powdered sugar

400 g (1 ¾ cups) sour cream, cold

Honey Cake Batter Directions:

1. Preheat oven to 320 degrees Fahrenheit.
2. Add honey to a medium size pot and heat on low heat until it just starts boiling, occasionally stirring.
3. Meanwhile, combine the eggs and sugar in mixer bowl fitted with a whisk attachment and whip on high speed until light and fluffy for about 5 minutes.
4. Once the honey starts boiling, add the baking soda while continuously whisking. The honey will then foam up, tripling in volume. Continue stirring until the honey darkens to an amber color, about 30 seconds. Add cubed butter and stir until it melts. Take off the heat and drizzle over the whipped eggs and sugar mixture while the mixer is running on low speed.
5. Add sifted flour in three additions while the mixer is still running on low. Once all flour has combined well with the wet ingredients—your honey batter is ready.
6. Line full baking sheet with parchment paper, lightly spray it with baking spray, pour the batter, and bake on middle rack for 6–8 minutes.
7. Once baked, allow it to fully cool off to room temperature before cutting out the circles.

Cream Filling Directions:

1. Add heavy cream and powdered sugar to the mixer bowl fitted with a whisk attachment and whip on high speed until it doubles in volume and forms soft peaks. Add sour cream and whip on low speed just until combined.

Assembly:

1. Using one inch (or the end of a large piping tip), 2 inch and 2.5-inches cookie cutters, cut out 10–12 circles of each size from the cooled honey sheet cake. Save the remaining cutouts for later.
2. Line each of the cupcake liners with piped cream first. Then follow with the smallest honey round, then a swirl of the cream, then the medium sized honey round. This should be followed by a swirl of cream, finishing with the largest 2.5-inch honey round and another swirl of piped cream.
3. Decorate as desired. My favorite way is to top these off with tangy and sweet berries, a drop of pure honey and the sprinkled powdered honey cake cutouts that you saved earlier.

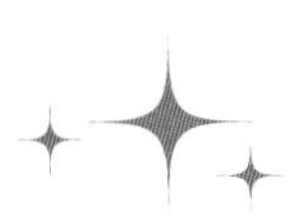

CHOCOLATE HONEY CAKE (CHOCOLATE MEDOVIK)

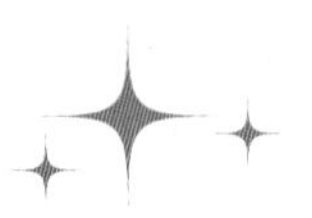

Who would I be if I hadn't made a chocolate version of one of my most favorite cakes? I cannot even describe in words how incredible this cake is. Just ask any of my friends or family. *PRO TIP: For Gluten Free version of this recipe, simply substitute the all-purpose flour with 1:1 Gluten Free flour.

CHOCOLATE HONEY CAKE:

85 g (4 Tbsp.) honey

1 tsp. baking soda

113 g ½ cup, 1 stick) unsalted butter, at room temperature

3 eggs, at room temperature

100 g (½ cup) granulated sugar

180 g (1 ½ cups) all-purpose flour

3 tsp. unsweetened cocoa powder

CREAM FILLING:

180 g (¾ cups) heavy cream, cold

85 g (¾ cup) powdered sugar

400 g (1 ¾ cups) sour cream, cold

GARNISH:

Fresh berries or chocolate shards

Honey Cake Batter Directions:

1. Preheat oven to 320 degrees Fahrenheit.
2. Add honey to a medium size pot and heat on low heat until it just starts to boil, occasionally stirring.
3. Meanwhile, combine the eggs and sugar in mixer bowl fitted with the whisk attachment and whip on high speed until light and fluffy for about 5 minutes.
4. Once the honey starts boiling, add the baking soda while continuously whisking. The honey will then foam up, tripling in volume. Continue stirring until the honey darkens to an amber color, about 30 seconds.
5. Add cubed butter and stir until it melts. Take off the heat and drizzle over the whipped egg and sugar mixture while the mixer is running on low speed.
6. Add sifted flour and cocoa powder in three additions while the mixer is still running on low. Once the dry ingredients have combined well with the wet ingredients - your chocolate honey batter is ready.
7. For this step I prefer to use the Wilton's Easy Layers Set in 8-inch size, filling each lightly greased cake pan with the honey batter. However, if you do not have these thin cake pans, here is another easy way: prepare 8 parchment paper sheets, each fitting your baking trays/sheets. Trace an 8-inch circle on each of the pieces of parchment paper. Use a plate or regular 8-inch baking pan as a guide. Spread the batter onto each traced circle with a silicone spatula. The batter shouldn't be too thin showing the parchment paper, nor should it be too thick to come off the traced line. Bake one or two trays at a time on the middle rack for 6–8 minutes.
8. Once baked, allow to fully cool off to room temperature before filling and stacking the cake. If desired, even out each baked layer by cutting out any uneven edges and saving the scraps. Process scraps in blender or food processor to a fine powder to be used for decorating the sides and top of the cake.

Cream Filling Directions:

1. Add heavy cream and powdered sugar to the mixer bowl fitted with the whisk attachment and whip on high speed until it doubles in volume and forms soft peaks. Add sour cream and whip on low speed just until combined.

Assembly:

1. Place a thin layer of the cream onto your 9- or 10-inch cake round/board. Follow with a chocolate honey cake layer, then pipe or spread about 3–5 tablespoons of the cream. Repeat with all the remaining layers of the cake and cream.
2. Place into the refrigerator for 30 minutes or freezer for 15 minutes to fully set before continuing with the decorations. Once filled cake has chilled in refrigerator or freezer, smooth out the remaining cream on top and sides of the cake, followed with the application/pressing of powdered cake scraps.
3. My favorite simple decorations for this cake are fresh berries or chocolate shards.

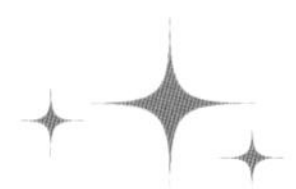

ANT HILL CAKE (MURAVEINIK)

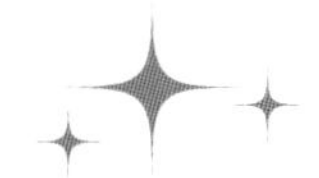

I like to say that I didn't just get to marry the most amazing human in the whole universe, but also got the best mother-in-law the world has seen. She has taught me many recipes and life hacks, as well as passing the torch of their families' traditions. This includes the recipe and the making of their families' signature, must have for all parties, The Muraveinik (The Ant Hill Cake). Don't be thrown off by its name—it is only a literal translation from our language and refers to the look of this cake. It is traditionally built into a tall cone shape and decorated with grated chocolate that resembles an ant hill with ants. If you like Dulce de Leche, walnuts, and crunchy cookie cakes—this cake is for you. *PRO TIP: For Gluten Free version of this recipe, simply substitute the all-purpose flour with 1:1 Gluten Free flour.

SWEET COOKIE DOUGH:

1 large egg

226 g (1 cup, 2 sticks) unsalted butter, cold

200 g (1 cup) granulated sugar

82 g (5 Tbsp.) whole milk

½ tsp. baking soda + 1 tsp. vinegar mixture

625 g (5 cups) all-purpose flour

DULCE DE LECHE FILLING:

794 (2 cans) of sweetened condensed milk

226 g (1 cup, 2 sticks) unsalted butter, at room temperature

200 g (2 cups) coarsely crushed walnuts

EGGLESS CONDENSED MILK BUTTERCREAM:

226 g (1 cup, 2 sticks) unsalted butter, at room temperature

397 g (1 cup + 2 Tbsp., 1 can) sweetened condensed milk, at room temperature

1 tsp. vanilla extract or emulsion

Cookie Directions:

1. Add all ingredients to the stand mixer bowl fitted with a pedal attachment and mix on low speed for approximately 5 minutes until the dough comes together/forms a ball.
2. Remove the dough from the bowl, wrap in kitchen plastic/cling film and refrigerate for 2 hours.
3. Preheat your oven to 375 degrees Fahrenheit.
4. After the dough has chilled in the refrigerator, cut it into several small pieces, and pass each piece through a meat grinder (for example, meat grinding stand mixer attachment), laying every layer of grinded dough flat on the baking sheet. This recipe should yield 2 baking pans/half sheets of "dough strings".
5. Bake one tray at a time on middle rack of your oven for 15–25 minutes until most of it turns a light golden color. Rotate your baking sheet halfway through the time.
6. Allow all baked dough to cool to room temperature, and then break it into small pieces the size of a grape or blueberry into a large bowl.

Dulce de Leche Filling Directions:

1. Making Dulce de Leche (This can be done way ahead of time, or right before starting to make the dough)
2. Place both cans of sweetened condensed milk into a large pot, fully cover them with water, cover the pot, and bring to a boil on high heat. Cans must be completely submerged in water.
3. Once the water is boiling, reduce the heat to low and continue boiling covered for exactly 2 hours. Make sure the water is still slightly boiling.
4. Once 2 hours have passed, carefully pour out the water from the pot, leaving the cans in, and add cold water leaving the cans to completely cool off. Sealed cans of this homemade Dulce de Leche can stay at room temperature for up to 30 days.
5. To make the filling: in a stand mixer fitted with pedal attachment, cream the cooled Dulce de Leche from both cans with room temperature butter on low speed until all combined and smooth. Be careful not to overmix.
6. Remove the bowl from the mixer and gently fold in coarsely crushed walnuts and broken cookie/pastry pieces.

Condensed Milk Buttercream Directions:

1. In the bowl of a mixer fitted with a whisk attachment, whip 1cup of room temperature butter for approximately 8 minutes until it has tripled in volume and become light and fluffy. Stop to scrape the bottom of the bowl a few times.
2. Add 1 teaspoon of vanilla extract or emulsion to the whipped butter.
3. Add 14 ounces sweetened condensed milk in thirds, whipping for about 8–10 seconds after each addition. Don't forget to scrape the bottom of the bowl after each addition.

Assembly:

1. Traditionally this famous Ukrainian "Ant Hill" cake is built by hand on a large plate or cake board into a tall pyramid/cone, resembling an ant hill. It is decorated with grated chocolate.
2. For my modern twist and the opportunity to complete the cake with other mediums, such as ganache, buttercreams, and even fondant it is best to stack this cake with my fill and peel technique.

34
THE WORLD'S FAIR
CAKE
His nine-year-old brother, Larry, looked in. His soon-to-be-
year-old sister, Sherry, peeked below Larry's arm. "Are
home, Pa?"
asked.
hot. I don't want

THE ULTIMATE KIEV CAKE (KIEVSKIY)

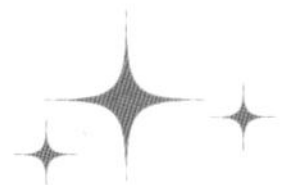

Kiev Cake (Kievskiy Tort) is an absolute staple in any former Soviet Union family. My husband still considers it his second favorite after "Muraveinik". Almost all generations of any eastern European family either does its best to make one at home or searches local eastern European grocery stores to buy one, hoping it tastes just as they remember it from their childhoods. The myth of the creation of first Kiev Cake and its original recipe is supposedly kept "under lock". My fond and nostalgic memories of Kiev Cake are forever connected to my grandma, who skillfully made this cake in her own kitchen for any special family occasions. I cherish this recipe and am sharing it with you with the utmost love.

MERINGUE CAKE LAYERS:

*NOTE: Separate 5 eggs, setting aside egg whites for meringue and egg yolks for buttercream

200 g egg whites (from approximately 6 eggs), at room temperature

250 g granulated sugar

250 g (2 cups) hazelnuts (can be substituted with cashew or almonds)

60 g (½ cup) all-purpose flour

KIEV BUTTERCREAM:

160 g (2.9 cups) whole milk, at room temperature

6 egg yolks, room temperature

160 g (¾ cups) granulated sugar

1 tsp. vanilla

¼ tsp. almond extract

30 g (4 Tbsp.) cocoa powder

GARNISH:

Gilded and roasted whole hazelnuts, chocolate shards, and bark

Meringue Cake Layers Directions:

1. Preheat oven to 270 degrees Fahrenheit. Place hazelnuts into a shallow skillet and roast on low heat, constantly mixing, until golden brown. If using hazelnuts with a skin, transfer roasted hazelnuts into a tea towel. Then cover and roll with pressure—the tea towel will remove the skin. Allow hazelnuts to cool and coarsely chop.
2. Alternatively, you can purchase roasted shelled and grated hazelnuts at a local grocery store.
3. Combine chopped hazelnuts and flour in a bowl, set aside.
4. Wipe the bowl and whisk attachment of the stand mixer with lemon juice or vinegar, removing any traces of oils or dust. Place your room temperature egg whites into the mixer bowl fitted with a whisk attachment. Start whipping the egg whites on low speed for approximately 1 minute, allowing bubbles to form. Slowly start increasing the mixer speed to medium. Continue whipping on medium speed for approximately 3 minutes until the meringue forms soft peaks.
5. While still whipping on medium speed, start drizzling the sugar onto the egg whites.
6. Once all the sugar is added, continue whipping the meringue for an additional 3 minutes until it forms hard peaks, becoming shiny and doubling in volume. The meringue should hold its form and have strong resistance when pushed with the whisk attachment or spatula.

7. Carefully and lightly fold the hazelnut flour mixture into the meringue in 3 steps, just until it's all combined.

8. Lightly spray two 8-inch spring forms or baking pans, line the bottom with parchment paper rounds and fill each with an even amount of hazelnut meringue mixture.

9. Bake at 270 degrees Fahrenheit for 2 hours. Once 2 hours have passed – allow the baked meringue cake layers to fully cool off in the closed oven for at least 1 hour, though overnight is best. Note: do not open the oven during baking and cooling time, otherwise your meringue may crack or not fully bake to the correct consistency.

10. Once baked meringue layers have fully cooled off in the oven for at least an hour, or overnight, remove them from the oven. Loosen up the sides of the meringue layers by running a knife alongside the spring form or your baking pans and then carefully extract the meringue from form/pan and remove parchment rounds. Trim the sides of both meringue cakes with serrated knife or grater, saving the crumbles for decorating. Set the cakes and crumbles aside. If the meringue cakes were prepared in advance, store them wrapped into parchment paper in a cool dry place such as a pantry.

Kiev Buttercream Directions:

1. Place milk into a medium sized pot and place it on medium heat.

2. Whisk the egg yolks and sugar in a separate medium sized pot and set aside.

3. Once the milk has warmed up and started developing rolling bubbles but is not boiling yet, remove from heat and slowly drizzle over continuously whisked egg yolk/sugar mixture.

4. Place this mixture onto a low heat, constantly whisking until the consistency resembles condensed milk/thickens. Remove from heat and set aside to cool until it is at room temperature.

5. Place the room temperature butter into a mixer bowl and whip it on high speed with a whisk attachment for at least 8 minutes until it doubles in volume, turns lighter in color, and become fluffy.

6. Reduce mixer speed to low and add vanilla extract. Increase mixer speed to high and continue whipping for an additional minute.

7. Reduce mixer speed to low again and slowly, in a steady thin stream, drizzle the egg yolk mixture over the whipped butter.

8. Once all the egg mixture is added, reduce the mixer speed to low and add almond extract. Allow it to incorporate on low speed for a few seconds.

9. Stop your mixer and remove approximately 1/3 of this prepared buttercream into a separate bowl. You will use it for filling the cake.

10. Add cocoa powder into the remaining 2/3 of buttercream and whip on low speed for an additional 2 minutes. Mix until all cocoa powder is well incorporated into the buttercream.

Assembly:

1. Place a small amount of chocolate buttercream onto your cake round/drum or serving platter, followed by the first layer of meringue cake with the smoothest/flattest side down. Place all of the white buttercream, smooth it out with off-set spatula, and cover with the second meringue cake layer. Place the filled cake into the refrigerator for 30 minutes.
2. After the cake has cooled and settled in refrigerator, cover the cake with the chocolate buttercream, smoothing and straightening the sides and top of the cake. Sprinkle or hand press the sides of the cake with the meringue crumbles and chopped hazelnuts (optional).
3. Traditionally the top of the cake is decorated with floral and leaf piped elements, resembling Kiev's famous chestnut trees. I love to decorate this cake with chocolate buttercream, piped with Wilton 8B tip, and gilded roasted whole hazelnuts.

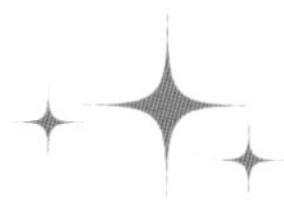

DULCE DE LECHE CAKE

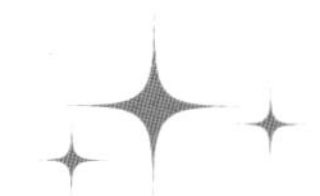

Ninety percent of eastern European classic desserts are made with Dulce de Leche. This cake is a song to my childhood, small town bakeries, and a complete ode to all Dulce de Leche filled and flavored desserts that I have grown up with. It has a modern twist: the tall 6-inch cake, the chocolate drip, and the gilded hazelnuts decorating it. *PRO TIP: For Gluten Free version of this recipe, simply substitute the all-purpose flour with 1:1 Gluten Free flour.

CAKE/FILLING:

113 g (½ cup, 1 stick) unsalted butter, at room temperature

400 g (1 ¾ cups) granulated sugar

115 g (½ cup) vegetable oil

500 g (3 cups + 2 Tbsp.) all-purpose flour

5 eggs, at room temperature

250 ml (1 cup) whole milk, at room temperature

1 tsp. baking powder

1 tsp. salt

1 Tbsp. vanilla (clear preferred, but not required)

2 cans sweetened condensed milk for Dulce de Leche (½ can for batter, ½ can for buttercream, 1 can for the filling)

DULCE DE LECHE BUTTERCREAM:

226 g (1 cup, 2 sticks) unsalted butter, at room temperature

14 oz (1 can) homemade Dulce de Leche, at room temperature

CONDENSED MILK BUTTERCREAM:

See page 8

GARNISH:

Gilded hazelnuts

Chocolate crunch pearls (optional)

Dulce de Leche Directions:

1. Dulce de Leche (This step can be done way ahead of time)
2. Place both cans of sweetened condensed milk into a large pot, fully cover them with water, cover the pot, and bring to a boil on high heat. Cans must be completely submerged in water.
3. Once the water is boiling, reduce the heat to low and continue boiling covered for exactly 2 hours. Make sure the water is still slightly boiling.
4. Once 2 hours have passed, carefully pour out the water from the pot, leaving the cans in, and add cold water leaving the cans to completely cool off. Sealed cans of this homemade Dulce de Leche can stay at room temperature for up to 30 days

Dulce de Leche Cake Layers Directions:

1. Preheat oven to 328 degrees Fahrenheit.
2. Place the oil, butter, and sugar into the stand mixer bowl. Fit the mixer with a whisk attachment and beat the above ingredients together for 5 minutes on high speed until the mixture becomes light and fluffy.
3. Reduce the mixer speed to low and add the eggs one at a time, scraping down the bowl in between each addition.
4. Sift the dry ingredient together and set aside. Combine the wet ingredients in a separate bowl and set aside.

5. While the mixer is still running on low speed, add the dry ingredients to the mixer, alternating with the wet. You want to have 3 parts dry and 2 parts wet ingredients.
6. Remove the bowl with the batter from the mixer and gently fold in ½ can of prepared/cooled Dulce de Leche. Avoid completely mixing in the Dulce de Leche into the batter. You want to see the ribbons of Dulce de Leche throughout the cake layers.
7. Fill your prepared (greased or lined) three 6-inch baking pans with the batter, 2/3 full.
8. Bake at 328 degrees Fahrenheit for 40–45 min until the inserted toothpick comes out dry and clean.
9. Cool on wire rack to room temperature; wrap, refrigerate or freeze before cutting each baked layer in half, resulting in 6 cake layers total.

Dulce de Leche Buttercream Directions:

1. In the bowl of a mixer fitted with a whisk attachment, whip the butter for approximately 8 minutes until it has tripled in volume and become light and fluffy. Stop to scrape the bottom of the bowl a few times.
2. Reduce the speed of the mixer to low and add the previously prepared and cooled homemade Dulce de Leche, in thirds, whipping for about 8–10 seconds after each addition. Don't forget to scrape the bottom of the bowl after each addition.

Assembly:

1. Place a small layer of condensed milk buttercream onto your 8-inch cake board/round.
2. Follow with a cake layer, a ring of condensed milk buttercream around the edges of the cake layer, and the Dulce de Leche buttercream in the center.
3. Optional: add chocolate crunch pearls. Follow with the next cake layer, a ring of condensed milk buttercream, and then the Dulce de Leche filling in the center, Repeat with the remaining cake layers and filling, alternating placing the dulce de leche buttercream and the dulce de leche filling.
4. Once cake has been filled, aligned, and straightened out, place into the refrigerator for 30 minutes to set.
5. Follow with a crumb coat and the final perfecting coats of dulce de leche buttercream, refrigerating after every coat.
6. Decorate with a simple chocolate ganache drip, gilded hazelnuts, and chocolate pearls.

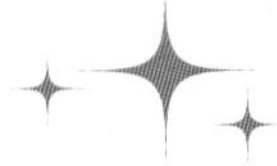

EGGLESS YOGURT CHERRY CAKE

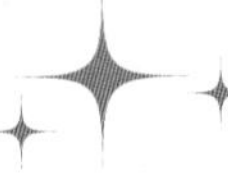

Even though my grandma made this cake with her homemade yogurt and powdered the granulated sugar in old fashioned coffee grinder, I can vouch that my rendition of it tastes exactly how I remember it. And aren't we lucky to be able to buy powdered sugar in grocery stores? But if you are ever out of it, just add the granulated sugar to food processor or blender and pulse until it magically turns into super fine powdered sugar, also known as confectionary sugar. *PRO TIP: For Gluten Free version of this recipe, simply substitute the all-purpose flour with 1:1 Gluten Free flour.

CAKE:

300 g (1 ¼ cups) plain Greek yogurt, at room temperature

450 g (3 ½ cups) self-rising flour

225 g (1 cup) granulated sugar

375 ml (1 ½ cups) whole milk, at room temperature

75 ml (2 ½ Tbsp.) vegetable oil

4 tsp. baking powder

1 tsp. vanilla

100 g (½ cup) fresh pitted or frozen pitted sweet cherries (can be substituted for canned, drained)

YOGURT FROSTING:

500 g (2 cups) plain Greek yogurt

2 tsp. pure vanilla extract

130 g (1 cup) powdered sugar

100 g (½ cups) fresh pitted or frozen cherries (can be substituted for canned, drained and dried)

CONDENSED MILK BUTTERCREAM:

See page 8

GARNISH:

Cherry marmalade squares

Cake Directions:

1. Preheat your oven to 325 degrees Fahrenheit.
2. In the bowl of a stand mixer fitted with a whisk attachment combine the yogurt and sugar and mix on low speed for approximately 8 minutes until smooth.
3. While mixer is still continuously mixing on low, sift in flour and baking powder and mix until combined.
4. Slowly pour in milk, vegetable oil, and vanilla while mixer is still whisking on low speed. Whisk until you have a smooth batter.
5. Lightly roll or dust drained/dried sweet cherries in flour, set aside.
6. Remove the bowl from stand mixer and gently fold floured sweet cherries.
7. Spray your 6-inch cake pans with non-stick baking spray or grease with butter and pour your cake batter in each pan.
8. Bake at 325 degrees Fahrenheit on the middle rack for 40–50 minutes until an inserted toothpick comes out clean and dry, with no wet crumbles on it. Make sure not to open your oven for the first 35 minutes, otherwise your cakes will not bake properly and will not rise.
9. Once your cake layers are baked, cool on wire rack upside down without removing the cake pans until they are cool to the touch. Once the cakes have cooled, wrap them in plastic wrap and either freeze or refrigerate them before stacking and decorating them.

Cherry Cream Directions:

1. Place a fine-mesh strainer over a small bowl. Place the yogurt in the strainer. Wrap with plastic wrap and place in the fridge to drain, at least two hours and preferably overnight. This step is important. Otherwise, the yogurt will be too watery and will not make a proper frosting.
2. Using a stand or hand mixer set on medium speed, beat together the strained yogurt, vanilla, and sugar until the frosting thickens, about 2 minutes.
3. Remove the mixer bowl from the stand mixer and set aside.
4. Puree the cherries in the food processor or blender.
5. Fold the cherry puree into the yogurt cream.
6. Cover and place it in the fridge for 30 minutes, while your baked cakes are cooling.

Assembly:

1. Place a small layer of Condensed Milk Buttercream onto your 8-inch cake board/ round. Follow with a cake layer, a ring of Condensed Milk Buttercream around the edges of the cake layer, and the cherry cream in the center.
2. Follow with the next cake layer, a buttercream ring, and the cherry cream. Repeat with the remaining cake layers and filling.
3. Once cake has been filled, aligned, and straightened out, place into the refrigerator for 30 minutes to set. Follow with a crumb coat and the final perfecting coats of Condensed Milk Buttercream, refrigerating after every coat.
4. Decorating possibilities for this cake are endless. I chose some simple piped rosettes and cherry marmalade squares from Trader Joe's.

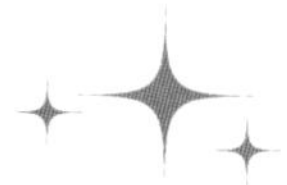

PEACH PASTRY COOKIES

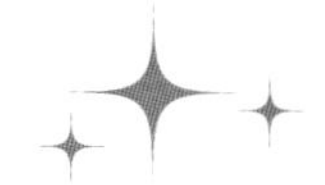

Peach Imposters Alert. Besides being incredibly cute and realistic looking, these pastry cookies are beyond delightful and taste nothing like peaches. They are a soft and fluffy cookie with Dulce de Leche filling and a whole almond in the center. Top them with fresh mint leaves and bring a full basket to any celebration to surprise and delight your family and friends. *PRO TIP: For Gluten Free version of this recipe, simply substitute the all-purpose flour with 1:1 Gluten Free flour.

COOKIES:

150 g (3/4 cups) granulated sugar

113 g (1/2 cup, 1 stick) unsalted butter, at room temperature

2 eggs, at room temperature

46 g (3 Tbsp.) sour cream

1 tsp. baking powder

312 g (2 1/2 cups) all-purpose flour

FILLING:

1 can sweetened condensed milk

50 g (1/3 cup) raw (or lightly roasted) whole almonds

GARNISH:

250 ml (1 cup) clear no pulp peach juice or apple juice, divided into 1/2 cup and 1/2 cup in separate bowls (you can also use any other no pulp juice of your choice).

Yellow and Red gel food coloring

100 g (1/2 cup) granulated sugar for decorations

Fresh mint leaves

Homemade Dulce de Leche Directions:

1. Place 1 can of sweetened condensed milk into the pot with water cover and bring to a boil on high heat. Water must completely cover the can of sweetened condensed milk.
2. Once the water starts boiling, reduce the heat to low keep the pot covered, and boil the can of sweetened condensed milk for precisely 2 hours. Make sure the water is still slightly bubbling on low heat.
3. Once 2 hours have passed, pour out the hot water from the pot carefully, keeping the can in the pot, pour cold water into the pot making sure the water is fully covering the can, and set aside to cool off.

Cookie Directions:

1. Prepare the mint leaves. Wash and pat dry, setting aside.
2. Place sugar, butter, and eggs into your mixer bowl, and stir with pedal attachment on low speed, slowly increasing the speed to high. Mix on high speed for about 5 minutes, until all the ingredients are combined and smooth.
3. Reduce the speed of your mixer to low and add sour cream, one tablespoon at a time. Mix on low speed until the sour cream is well combined, then slowly increase the mixer speed to high and beat the mixture for about 1 minute.
4. Reduce mixer speed to low and slowly add baking powder and flour, while still mixing on low speed until flour has fully incorporated.

5. As soon as all flour is added and has fully incorporated into the wet ingredients—turn off your mixer, be careful to not overmix. The dough should be sticky and pliable.
6. Cover the bowl with the dough with cling film/Glade and refrigerate for 20 minutes.
7. Meanwhile, preheat your oven to 395 degrees Fahrenheit.
8. Line your baking pan/cookie sheet with parchment paper, set aside.
9. Prepare the decorations. Add a few drops of yellow gel food coloring into one bowl with peach or apple juice, and a few drops of red food coloring into another bowl of peach or apple juice. You can also use any other no pulp clear juice of your choice. Stir in gel food colors well until they fully dissolve in your juice. Set aside.
10. At this time, the dough has cooled off in the fridge. Prepare your parchment paper lined baking sheet, teaspoon, and small bowl with some water. You can also wear gloves to avoid the dough sticking to your hands. Dip one hand in water and take 1 full teaspoon of the dough and roll a small ball the size of a whole walnut. Place this on the parchment paper on the baking sheet. Make sure your balls of dough are at least half an inch apart, as they will expand during baking.
11. Bake on the middle rack of your oven for 15 minutes, turning around the baking sheet halfway to allow even baking.
12. Allow baked cookies to cool off for a few minutes.

Assembly:

1. Once the baked cookies have cooled off, scoop out a center from each cookie using a teaspoon or melon baller. Optional: reserve the scooped out centers to later mix into the Dulce de Leche.
2. By this time your homemade Dulce de Leche has cooled off in cold water.
3. Fill each cookie with approximately one teaspoon of Dulce de Leche and one whole almond.
4. Try to match each half of the peach cookie in size/shape, stick each half together, forming a peach.
5. Once all halves of the cookies are matched, freeze them for about 10 minutes—so they adhere together and don't move too much during decorating.
6. Once filled/matched cookies have chilled in the freezer, it's time to decorate.
7. Set bowls with yellow and red juice, a bowl with granulated sugar, whole almonds, and mint. Dip half of each peach cookie into red apple juice, the other half into yellow apple juice, and then roll in sugar. Add one or a couple of fresh mint leaves.
8. Once all peach cookies have been decorated, you are free to enjoy them immediately. They do taste best after being refrigerated for a few hours, but who's going to wait?

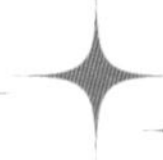

GRANDMA'S ROSE MERINGUE COOKIES

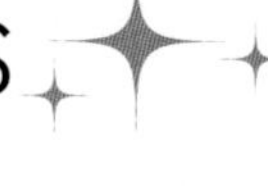

Ah, these Rose Meringue Cookies have such a special story. My paternal grandma made them for me every weekend when I visited during summer school break and served them with her signature homemade hot chocolate. Traditionally the meringue isn't colored, but I want to aim for these to be as close to the rose's look as possible. A drop of pink food coloring is completely optional. *PRO TIP: For Gluten Free version of this recipe, simply substitute the all-purpose flour with 1:1 Gluten Free flour.

COOKIES:

375 g (3 cups) all-purpose flour

226 g (2 cups, 4 sticks) unsalted butter, at room temperature

240 g (1 cup) sour cream, at room temperature

3 large eggs, at room temperature (yolks and whites separated)

300 g (1 ½ cups) granulated sugar

1 tsp. baking soda + 1 tsp. vinegar mixture

125 g (1 cup) of finely crushed raw walnuts

Cookie Directions:

1. Preheat oven to 350 degrees Fahrenheit.
2. In a stand mixer fitted with a pedal attachment, combine and mix the butter and flour on low speed for about 3 minutes until the mixture resembles a crumble.
3. While the mixer is still going on low speed, add the sour cream and baking soda/vinegar mixture. Continue mixing on low speed until smooth for about 1 minute.
4. Separate the egg yolks and reserve the whites. Add 3 egg yolks to the dough and continue mixing on low speed for about 1 minute until well combined.

5. Turn off the mixer and transfer your dough to a piece of well-floured parchment paper. The dough should look pliable, slightly sticky, and not be rubbery at this point. Lightly flour your hands and divide the dough into 3 equal parts. Wrap each piece into plastic wrap and refrigerate for 30 minutes.

6. Meanwhile prepare the meringue. Add your egg whites and sugar to the clean, degreased bowl of your stand mixer fitted with a whisk attachment. I recommend wiping the bowl with a bit of vinegar or lemon juice first.

7. Start whipping your egg whites/sugar mixture on low speed, slowly increasing the speed of the mixer to high. Keep mixing on high for about 8 minutes or until the meringue achieves stiff peaks.

8. Once the dough has chilled in refrigerator for 30 minutes, roll each of the 3 pieces into a thin rectangle to about 3 mm thickness. It is easier to do so in between two well-floured pieces of parchment paper.

9. With your offset spatula, spread about 1/3 of your meringue over the rolled dough and sprinkle with walnuts.

10. Roll the meringue cookie dough into a loose cylinder shape. Starting from the narrower end, wrap it into parchment paper and refrigerate for 30 minutes. After, using a thread or floss, cut 2–3 cm pieces. Place each of the cut "roses" onto a baking sheet/pan lined with baking paper, flatter side of the cookie down. Make sure to leave about an inch of distance between each cookie.

11. Repeat with remaining dough and meringue.

12. Bake one baking sheet/tray at a time on 350 degrees Fahrenheit for 25–30 minutes on the middle rack. Refrain from opening the oven for at least the first 20 minutes.

13. Allow baked rose meringue cookies to fully cool before removing them from parchment paper.

14. Optional: dust with powdered sugar, powdered freeze-dried raspberries or strawberries.

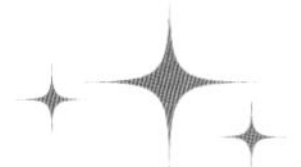

MOM'S ZEBRA BUNDT CAKE

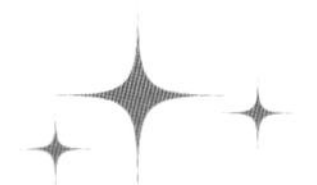

This Zebra Bundt Cake is most likely the first baking project I learned from my mom. She is an absolute master of the Bundt cakes and has amazing tricks for releasing them properly. This cake is a dense, yet airy combination of sweet chiffon and chocolate batter, topped with a simple yet decadent glaze. *PRO TIP: For Gluten Free version of this recipe, simply substitute the all-purpose flour with 1:1 Gluten Free flour.

ZEBRA CAKE:

5 eggs, at room temperature

300 g (1 ½ cups) granulated sugar

113 g (½ cup, 1 stick) melted and cooled butter

240 g (1 cup) full-fat sour cream or Greek yogurt

240 g all-purpose flour

1 tsp. baking powder

2 Tbsp. cocoa powder

CHOCOLATE GLAZE:

2 Tbsp. milk

1 Tbsp. cocoa powder

1 Tbsp. granulated sugar

GARNISH:

Microgreens, edible flowers, nuts of choice, and freeze-dried fruits if desired

Zebra Cake Directions:

1. Preheat your oven to 320 degrees Fahrenheit.
2. Add eggs, sugar, melted cooled butter, and sour cream into the bowl of stand mixer fitted with a whisk attachment and whip on low speed, slowly increasing to the highest speed for 5 minutes.
3. Reduce the speed of the mixer to low and slowly drizzle sifted flour and baking powder into the whipped wet ingredients.
4. Continue mixing on low speed until all the flour is incorporated and the batter resembles the consistency of sour cream
5. Separate the batter into two equal parts in separate bowls and add cocoa powder to one half.
6. Optional: add orange zest, raisins, or nuts of your choice.
7. Grease your Bundt cake pan. I prefer using Wilton's Bake Easy Spray. Alternatively, you can grease the pan with a cube of butter. Pour the batter into a greased pan alternating the white and chocolate. Swirl the batter lightly with a knife or a toothpick.
8. Bake at 320 degrees Fahrenheit on the middle rack for 30–35 minutes or until an inserted toothpick comes out clean with no wet crumbs on it. Do not open the oven for the first 30 minutes; otherwise your cake may not rise.
9. The secret to releasing your baked Bundt cakes successfully and easily: as soon as the cake has fully baked, take it out of the oven and flip it upside down onto the cooling rack. Do not remove the Bundt cake pan just yet. Take two kitchen or tea towels, dip them in cold water, squeeze out the excess, and immediately put over the Bundt pan making sure the whole pan is covered including the center. When towels turn hot, repeat the above steps 2–3 times. Once the towel tricks are complete, allow the pan to continue cooling off to room temperature before removing the Bundt pan.
10. Transfer the cooled baked Zebra Cake onto your cake board or serving platter.
11. Prepare the chocolate glaze.

Chocolate Glaze Directions:

1. Add the milk, cocoa powder, and sugar into a small pot and place on low heat, continuously mixing. As soon as the glaze starts lightly boiling—remove it from heat and pour it over the Bundt cake.

Assembly:

1. Decorate with microgreens, edible flowers, nuts of choice, and freeze-dried fruits if desired.
2. This delicious and scrumptious Zebra Cake can be served immediately or can be refrigerated overnight in an airtight container.

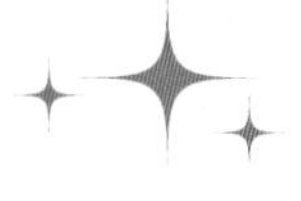

EGGLESS SUGAR-FREE BERRY PASSIONFRUIT PAVLOVA

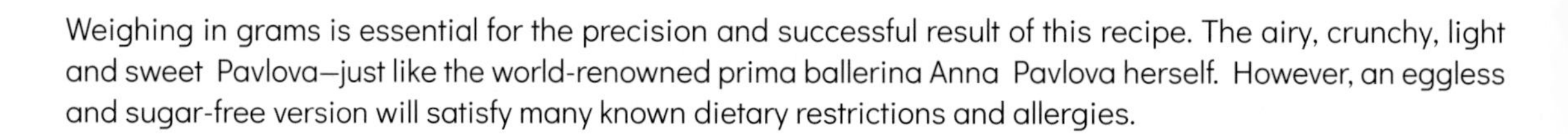

Weighing in grams is essential for the precision and successful result of this recipe. The airy, crunchy, light and sweet Pavlova—just like the world-renowned prima ballerina Anna Pavlova herself. However, an eggless and sugar-free version will satisfy many known dietary restrictions and allergies.

MERINGUE:

150 g aquafaba, at room temperature

pinch of salt

150 g monk sugar

2 tsp. cornstarch

1 tsp. white wine vinegar

½ tsp. of pure vanilla extract

PASSIONFRUIT CHANTILLY CREAM:

250 g of cold heavy cream (can be substituted with dairy-free creams)

50 g of powdered monk sugar

½ tsp. of pure vanilla extract

100 g passionfruit puree, fresh or frozen

MIXED BERRY REDUCTION:

100 g fresh strawberries, hulled and sliced

100 g fresh blueberries

100 g fresh blackberries

100 g fresh raspberries

1 tsp. of fresh or bottled lemon or lime juice

1 Tbsp. of powdered monk sugar (optional)

GARNISH:

Fresh berries

Meringue Directions:

1. Preheat your oven to 180 degrees Fahrenheit. Place a sheet of parchment paper on a sheet pan and draw an 8-inch circle on the paper. Drawing a circle around your 8-inch cake pan works best.
2. To make the meringue: place the aquafaba and salt in the bowl of a stand mixer fitted with a whisk attachment. Beat first on low speed until bubbles form, and then gradually increase speed to high and mix on high speed for about 1 minute until firm. With the mixer still on high, slowly add the sugar and beat for about 2 minutes or until it makes firm, shiny peaks.
3. Remove the bowl from the mixer, sift the cornstarch onto the meringue, sprinkle white wine vinegar and vanilla, and fold them in lightly with a rubber spatula. Pile the meringue into the middle of the circle on the parchment paper and smooth it within the circle, forming a thick pie like tall disc. Bake for 1½ hours without opening oven. Turn off the oven, keep the door closed, and allow the meringue to cool completely in the oven for 2 hours or overnight.
4. Once baked Pavlova has rested in the closed oven for at least 2 hours, transfer it onto a cake stand or plate.

Passionfruit Chantilly Cream Directions:

1. Add cold heavy cream, powdered monk sugar, and vanilla into your mixer bowl. Place into a mixer fitted with a whisk attachment and start mixing on low speed until all the sugar and the heavy cream are fully combined. Slowly increase the speed of your mixer to medium.
2. Once the cream starts thickening, increase the speed of the mixer to high, and mix until the cream doubles in volume and the whisk creates ruffle like indentations. It's important to immediately stop at this point. Otherwise you will end up with butter.
3. Fold the passionfruit puree into the whipped cream by hand but avoid overmixing.

Mixed Berry Reduction Directions:

1. Combine strawberries, blueberries, blackberries, raspberries, lemon juice, and sugar in a small pot and mix well. Place on low/medium heat, allowing it to start to boil.
2. Reduce heat to low, mixing well and cook/reduce for 5 minutes. Remove from the heat, immediately transfer to a heatproof large bowl, cover it with kitchen wrap, and place it into the refrigerator for 15 minutes.

Assembly:

1. Fill Pavlova with Passionfruit Chantilly Cream and Berry Reduction.
2. Refrigerate for at least 1 hour before serving.
3. Garnish with fresh berries. This is best served within 24 hours of making.

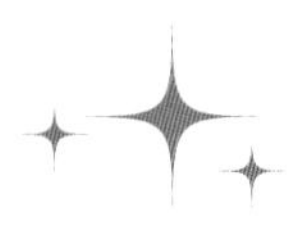

SUGAR-FREE MERINGUE SEASHELL TREATS

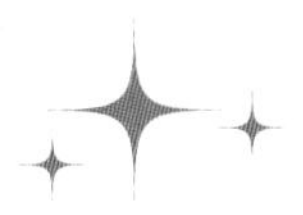

Weighing in grams is essential for the precision and successful result of this recipe.

MERINGUE:

*NOTE: Separate your egg whites from the egg yolks while your eggs are cold. Leave the egg whites out to warm up to room temperature for at least an hour.

*NOTE: To make the superfine monk sugar, pulse monk sugar in your blender just a few times.

100 g fresh egg whites, at room temperature

100 g super fine monk sugar

SUGAR-FREE BUTTERCREAM:

See page 11

GARNISH:

Optional: macarons see chapter 5

Meringue Directions:

1. Preheat your oven on the convectional bake setting at 200 degrees Fahrenheit.
2. Prepare a double boiler. I use a pot slightly larger in diameter than my mixing bowl. Fill it with a bit of water and place on medium-high heat.
3. Wipe your mixing bowl and whisk attachment with a bit of lemon juice on a piece of paper towel. Pour your room temperature egg whites and superfine monk sugar into your mixing bowl and place into a pot with boiling water. Make sure that your mixing bowl with egg whites and sugar does not touch the boiling water. Reduce the heat to medium-low to ensure that the water is barely simmering.
4. Whisk your egg whites/sugar mixture with your whisk nonstop for 2.5-3 minutes. I use the whisk mixer attachment—fewer steps, fewer dishes to wash.
5. Transfer your mixing bowl onto the mixer and start mixing on low speed for 30 seconds, gradually increasing the speed to high. Mix on high for 8 minutes. You are looking for stiff meringue here. Meaning when 8 minutes have passed pull your whisk out and check the meringue's peak—it should just slightly curve.
6. Place the meringue into your piping bag fitted with a Wilton's 8B piping tip. I prefer to use silicone baking mats for baking the meringue, but you can also use parchment paper. Here is a little tip to prevent your parchment paper from sliding on your baking tray when you pipe meringue—put a little drop or swipe of your meringue onto the baking tray under the parchment paper.
7. Pipe 3 long "tear drops" to form each half of the seashell.
8. Bake for 60 minutes on the middle rack. Meringues are ready when you slightly push on them and they do not move. If they are still wiggly, they need to be baked for a few more minutes.
9. Allow your meringue to fully cool off before removing them from your silicone mats or parchment paper. They can be eaten immediately or stored in an airtight container in a dark, dry, cool place for up to a month.

Assembly:

1. To fill and decorate: pipe dollops of sugar-free buttercream on each half of the meringue seashell, add a macaron (if using), and adhere both sides of the seashell tightly touching on one end to form a full "seashell."

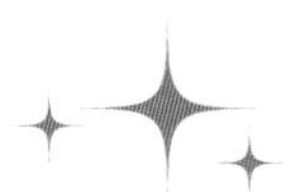

GELATIN-FREE MARSHMALLOWS (ZEFIR)

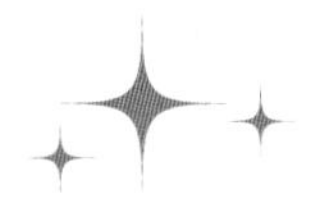

Weighing in grams is essential for precision and a successful result of this recipe.

Another mega famous dessert from my childhood that still delights the bakers and consumers in most parts of the world. I guarantee that you will fall in love with this treat. I encourage you to play with the piping tips. The possibilities for the design of these Zefir Marshmallows are endless.

MARSHMALLOW:

200 g apple puree

50 g sour cherry puree

200 g granulated sugar

1 egg white, at room temperature

SYRUP:

350 g granulated sugar

160 g water

8 g agar powde

GARNISH:

Powdered Sugar

Marshmallow & Syrup Directions:

1. Place the sugar, apple and cherry purees into a medium size pot over low heat, occasionally stirring. Reduce until the sugar completely melts. Remove the pot from the heat and set aside to cool off to room temperature.

2. Once the sugar/fruit puree mixture cools off to room temperature—transfer it into your mixer bowl, fitted with a whisk attachment.

3. To make the syrup: add the other 350 g of sugar, agar powder and water into a separate small pot, place on medium heat and while occasionally stirring—bring to a boil. Then reduce the heat to low and continue heating until the agar mixture gets to 230 degrees Fahrenheit on sugar thermometer.

4. While your agar/sugar syrup is heating, add the egg white to the fruit/sugar puree. Start mixing on low speed (for about 1 minute). Slowly increase the speed to medium and allow the mixture to whip on medium speed for about 3 minutes until the whisk attachment leaves stable, not runny streaks.

5. By this time the agar mixture should reach the required temperature. Take the pot off the heat and set aside. Once the agar mixture stops bubbling—start adding it to the fruit puree mixture in a slow thin stream, while the mixer is still running on medium speed. Make sure to add the agar stream to the side of the bowl or on the puree, never over the whisk attachment.

6. Once all the agar mixture is added to the fruit puree, increase the speed of your mixer to medium-high and continue whipping the marshmallow until it reaches stiff peaks.

7. While the mallow is getting to stiff peaks, prepare the baking sheets, trays lined with parchment paper or silicone mats, and fit your piping bag with your favorite large piping tip. I prefer to use Wilton 8B, 1M and 1D.

8. As soon as the marshmallow mixture reaches stiff peaks, transfer it into your piping bags fitted with piping tips. Do not leave the marshmallow mixture in the mixer bowl as agar sets fairly quickly.

9. Pipe your desired size of marshmallow swirls (rosettes) onto your earlier prepared parchment paper or silicone mats. Sizes may vary from 1 to 2 inches in diameter, or even larger.

10. Set the trays/pans aside for at least 4–5 hours.

Assembly:

1. After 5 hours, dust the top of each marshmallow half with powdered sugar, and adhere the two halves together if desired.

2. Store in an air-tight container in a cool, dry place.

CHAPTER 4

Cake Magic

CAKE IT WITH A FLAIR: MY ULTIMATE, GO-TO, FAVORITE, TRUE AND TESTED, 17 COMPLETE RECIPES, INCLUDING A SUGAR-FREE MEDOVIK

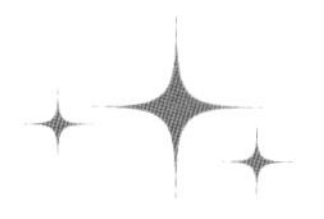

MY BEST MOIST AND FLUFFY VANILLA CAKE

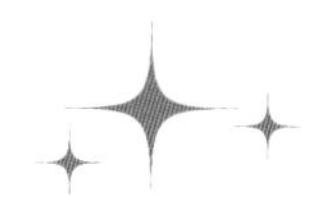

The classic Vanilla Cake, the staple for any baker, the possible struggle for any baker. The search of that best Vanilla Cake Recipe that is not too sweet, not too dense, flavorful, moist, airy, rises well, doesn't crumble too much, suitable for even the tallest tiered cake might take years. But your search is now over—I did the recipe testing, experimenting, developing, and this is an absolute WINNER. Even the toughest critics, my picky eaters: husband and middle son, are in love with this vanilla cake and request it to be made repeatedly. This Vanilla Cake recipe is versatile and can easily be adapted to other flavors, such as almond, lemon, coconut, and many more.

Weighing in grams is best for precision and a successful result of this recipe. *PRO TIP: For Gluten Free version of this recipe, simply substitute the all-purpose flour with 1:1 Gluten Free flour.

VANILLA CAKE:

135 g (2/3 cup) unsalted butter, at room temperature

450 g (2 ½ cups) granulated sugar

115 g (8 ½ Tbsp.) vegetable oil

5 eggs, at room temperature

500 g (3 cups + 2 Tbsp.) all-purpose flour

250 ml (1 cup) whole milk, at room temperature

1 tsp. baking powder

1 tsp. salt

1 Tbsp. clear vanilla (clear is preferred, but not required)

SWISS MERINGUE BUTTERCREAM:

300 g (from 9 eggs) fresh or carton egg whites

250 g (1 ¼ cups) caster (superfine) sugar

¼ tsp. salt

565 g (2 ½ cups, 5 sticks) unsalted butter, at room temperature

1 tsp. clear vanilla, lemon, or almond extract

Vanilla Cake Directions:

1. Preheat oven to 325 degrees Fahrenheit.Place the oil, butter, and sugar into the stand mixer bowl. Fit the mixer with a whisk attachment and beat the above ingredients together for 5 minutes on high speed. Mix until the mixture becomes light and fluffy.
2. Reduce the mixer speed to low and add the eggs one at a time, scraping down the bowl in between each addition.
3. Sift the dry ingredient together and set aside. Combine the wet ingredients in a separate bowl and set aside.
4. While the mixer is still running on low speed, add the dry ingredients to the mixer, alternating with the wet. You want to have 3 parts dry, and 2 parts wet ingredients.
5. Fill your prepared (greased or lined) 6-inch baking pans with the batter, 2/3 full.
6. Bake at 325 degrees Fahrenheit for 40–45 min until an inserted toothpick comes out dry and clean.
7. Cool on a wire rack, upside down, with the cake pans intact until the cakes chill to room temperature. Wrap into plastic wrap/cling film and either refrigerate for a few hours before use or freeze overnight to ease the cake filling, decorating, and stacking process. Trim and torte cold cake layers if needed before filling/assembling the cake.

Swiss Meringue Buttercream Directions:

1. Prepare a double boiler. Use a pot slightly larger in diameter than your mixing bowl. Fill it with a bit of water and place on medium-high heat.

2. Wipe your mixing bowl and whisk attachment with a bit of lemon juice or vinegar on a piece of paper towel. Place your egg whites, caster sugar and salt into your mixing bowl and place the mixing bowl into the pot with boiling water. Make sure that your mixing bowl with egg whites and sugar does not touch the boiling water. Reduce the heat to medium-low to ensure that the water is barely simmering.

3. Whisk your egg white/sugar mixture with your whisk nonstop for about 1 minute or until your sugar thermometer reaches 140 degrees Fahrenheit/60 degrees Celsius. I use the whisk mixer attachment—fewer steps, fewer dishes to wash. Check mixture with your fingers—you should not be feeling any grains of sugar.

4. Transfer your mixing bowl to a stand mixer and start mixing on low speed, gradually increasing the speed to high. Mix on high for 8 minutes until there are stiff peaks, meaning—when 8 minutes have passed, pull your whisk out and check the meringue's peak—it should just slightly curve.

5. Decrease mixer speed to medium and slowly add your 565 grams of unsalted butter, 1 tablespoon at a time. Then add 1 teaspoon of clear vanilla (or any other) extract and mix on high speed for 4 minutes. At some point you might be seeing that your buttercream is looking soupy—do not panic. As you continue adding butter while mixing, consistency will change.

6. Once 4 minutes have passed, decrease mixer speed to low and continue mixing for 2–4 minutes or longer, when possible, otherwise your Swiss Meringue Buttercream will have a lot of bubbles.

7. For this cake I chose to keep the natural color of the buttercream. However, if you are aiming for a snow-white color then add 1 drop of purple food coloring to cancel out any yellow.

Assembly:

1. Place a thin layer of buttercream onto your 8-inch cake board/round. Follow with placement of a cake layer, lightly pressing to help it adhere to the buttercream and cake round. Smooth out approximately ¼ to half a cup of buttercream. Repeat with the remaining cake layers and frosting.

2. Once the cake has been filled, aligned, and straightened out, place into the refrigerator for 30 minutes to set. Follow with a crumb coat, then final perfecting coats of the buttercream, refrigerating after every coat. Decorate as desired.

3. I chose a classic simple clean look for this cake, with a lightly offset spatula swirled cake top and rough edges.

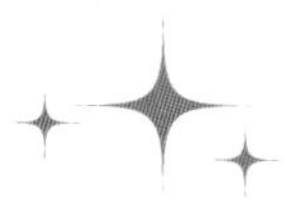

COCONUT RASPBERRY CAKE

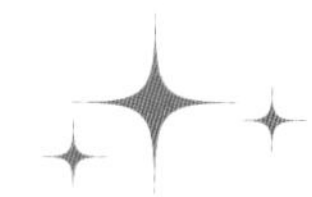

This cake is my ode to the limited-edition Raspberry Rafaello truffles that appeared in my local grocery store for a moment but brought so much joy as my occasional guilty pleasure treat. I am a huge fan of Rafaello to begin with, ever since I was a teenager. You have probably noticed by now—"berry" should have been my middle name as they are a big part of most of my desserts. Can you imagine my excitement when these raspberry coconut truffles appeared in stores? I had to make a cake inspired by them—even if you are not a fan of coconut—I guarantee you will fall in love with this cake. Lightly coconut flavored airy cake layers, raspberry buttercream (no food coloring added), coconut and raspberry condensed milk filling, and almond slivers make it delicious.

Weighing in grams is essential for the precision and successful result of this recipe. *PRO TIP: For Gluten Free version of this recipe, simply substitute the all-purpose flour with 1:1 Gluten Free flour.

COCONUT CAKE:

285 g (2 ⅓ cups) all-purpose flour

2 tsp. baking powder

½ tsp. baking soda

1 tsp. salt

170 g (12 Tbsp.) unsalted butter, at room temperature

330 g (1.4 cups) granulated sugar

5 large egg whites, at room temperature

120 g (½ cup) sour cream, at room temperature

2 tsp. pure vanilla extract

1 tsp. coconut extract

125 ml (½ cup) canned coconut milk, at room temperature

70 g (1 cup) shredded unsweetened coconut

FILLING:

3–6 Tbsp. of powdered freeze-dried raspberries (for the raspberry buttercream)

70 g (1 cup) shredded unsweetened coconut (for the coconut buttercream)

raw or lightly roasted unsalted almond slivers

50 g (10 Tbsp.) of finely chopped fresh or freeze-dried raspberries

RASPBERRY SWISS MERINGUE BUTTERCREAM:

For edges filling and frosting—see complete recipe for the original SMBC on page 14 chapter 2. Add 3–6 tablespoons of powdered freeze-dried raspberries.

COCONUT CONDENSED MILK BUTTERCREAM:

For main/center filling—see a complete recipe on page 8, chapter 2. Fold in shredded coconut.

GARNISH:

Coarsely chopped freeze-dried raspberries

Coconut slivers

Almond slivers,

Raspberry Macarons (optional)

Coconut Cake Directions:

1. Preheat oven to 325 degrees Fahrenheit. Grease/spray two 8-inch cake pans.
2. Whisk flour, baking powder, baking soda, and salt together. Set aside.
3. Using a stand mixer fitted with a whisk attachment, beat the butter and sugar together on medium-high speed for about 5 minutes or until smooth and creamy. Scrape down the sides and the bottom of the bowl with a silicone spatula as needed.
4. Beat in the egg whites until combined, and then add the sour cream, vanilla extract, and coconut extract. Beat until combined. Mixture will look curdled as a result of the varying textures and solid butter combining, which is completely normal. Scrape down the sides and the bottom of the bowl as needed.
5. With the mixer on low speed, slowly add the dry ingredients alternating with coconut milk. You want to have 3 parts dry and 2 parts wet. Mix on low speed until combined, and then fold in the shredded coconut with a silicone spatula. Mix it all by hand with a silicone spatula to make sure that there are no butter lumps at the bottom of the bowl. The batter will be slightly thick.
6. Pour batter evenly into the greased cake pans. Weigh them to ensure accuracy, if desired. Bake on the middle rack for 40–50 minutes or until the cakes are fully baked and an inserted toothpick comes out dry and clean. Do not open the oven the first 30 minutes or your cakes will not rise.
7. Allow cakes to cool completely in the pans set on a cooling rack upside down. Wrap cooled cakes into the kitchen plastic/cling film and either refrigerate for at least a few hours before use, or freeze overnight for easy, mess free frosting.

Assembly:

1. Once the cake layers have cooled in the refrigerator or freezer, trim and torte if needed, resulting in 4 cake layers.
2. Place a thin layer of raspberry buttercream onto your 10-inch cake board/round. Follow with the placement of a coconut cake layer, lightly pressing to help it adhere to the buttercream and cake round.
3. Pipe a tall ring of raspberry buttercream along the edges of the cake layer. Smooth out approximately ¼ to half a cup of coconut buttercream, followed by sprinkling chopped fresh or freeze-dried raspberries and almonds. Repeat with the remaining cake layers and filling.
4. Once the cake has been filled, aligned, and straightened out, place it into the refrigerator for 30 minutes to set. Follow with a crumb coat, final perfecting coats of the raspberry buttercream, refrigerating after every coat.
5. Decorate with coarsely chopped freeze-dried raspberries, coconut and almond slivers, and top with my Raspberry Macarons if desired. (Page 138, chapter 5)

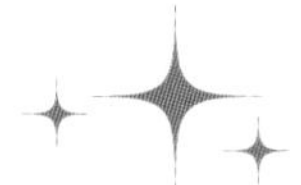

FERRERO ROCHER INSPIRED CAKE

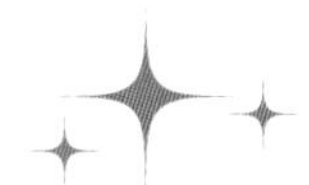

This cake is for all the Ferrero Rocher, chocolate, and meringue lovers. From the chocolatiest cake layers to the silky chocolate buttercream, chocolate ganache filling and the chocolate meringue crunch—this cake will not leave you dissatisfied.

Weighing in grams is essential for the precision and successful result of this recipe. *PRO TIP: For Gluten Free version of this recipe, simply substitute the all-purpose flour with 1:1 Gluten Free flour.

CHOCOLATE CAKE:

200 g (¾ cup) unsalted butter, at room temperature

400 g (2 cups) granulated sugar

4 large eggs, at room temperature

410 g (1 ¾ cups) hot strong coffee or expresso

100 g (0.9 cups) unsweetened cocoa powder

350 g (2 ¾ cups) all-purpose flour

1 tsp. salt

1 Tbsp. vanilla extract

1 ½ tsp. baking soda

1 tsp. baking powder

CHOCOLATE GANACHE:

90 g (½ cup) semi-sweet chocolate

30 g (6 tsp.) cold heavy cream (well shaken)

FILLING:

250 g (1 cup) Nutella

250 g (2 cups) lightly roasted coarsely crushed unsalted hazelnuts

4 Tbsp. of strong coffee or expresso (optional)

EGGLESS CHOCOLATE FROSTING:

Recipe on page 12 of Chapter 2

GARNISH:

Lightly warm chocolate ganache drip

Chocolate shards

Crushed chocolate meringue from page 175 in chapter 6.

Chocolate Cake Directions:

1. Preheat oven to 325 degrees Fahrenheit.
2. Sift your flour, baking soda, baking powder, and salt into a bowl and whisk them together. Set it aside.
3. Prepare coffee or expresso and whisk it well with cocoa powder until the cocoa dissolves completely. Set it aside to cool slightly. If desired, substitute hot water for coffee/espresso.
4. In a stand mixer fitted with a whisk attachment, whip the butter and sugar at medium speed for about 8–10 minutes or until light and fluffy.
5. Add eggs to the sugar mixture, one at a time, and blend them until incorporated. Scrape down the sides and bottom of the bowl as needed.
6. Add dry ingredients alternatively with warm cocoa/coffee mixture. Begin by adding dry, and then alternate with wet.
7. Spray four 6-inch baking pans with baking spray and fill with batter 2/3 of the way. Tap them on the table to knock out the air and bake at 325 degrees Fahrenheit for 45–50 minutes or until an inserted toothpick comes out clean. Allow them to cool for 10 minutes before removing from the baking pans onto a wire cooling rack.
8. Once cooled, wrap in kitchen plastic and place in the refrigerator or freezer overnight.

Chocolate Ganache Directions:

1. Place your chocolate and heavy cream in a microwave safe container, microwave in 30 seconds intervals, vigorously mixing the ganache in between heating sessions. Once all the chocolate has melted and combined well with heavy cream—set aside to cool to room temperature, occasionally whisking.

Assembly:

1. Place your cake board/drum on a rotating cake stand and smooth on a small amount of chocolate buttercream.
2. Place the first chocolate cake layer on a cake board, if desired. Sprinkle 1 tablespoon of coffee or expresso. With a piping bag fitted with a round piping tip (or tipless) and chocolate buttercream, pipe a thin tall ring of chocolate buttercream along the edge of the cake. This will work as a glue for your fillings and the following cake layers.
3. Smooth out approximately 2 tablespoons of Nutella over the cake layer inside the ring of the chocolate buttercream, followed by 2 tablespoons of crushed hazelnuts and 2–4 tablespoons of chocolate ganache. Place the next chocolate cake layer over this, aligning and lightly pressing with a bottom cake layer.
4. Repeat with the remaining cake layers, buttercream, and fillings. Smooth out the sides of the assembled cake with an offset spatula and place it into a freezer for 15 minutes or a refrigerator for 30 minutes.
5. Proceed to crumb coat your chilled cake with the remaining chocolate buttercream.
6. The possibilities of decorating this delicious cake are endless. I chose to leave it in a semi-naked rustic finish, followed by a lightly warm chocolate ganache drip, chocolate shards, and crushed chocolate meringue from page 175 in chapter 6.

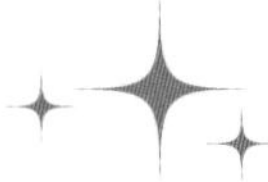

RAFAELLO INSPIRED COCONUT CAKE

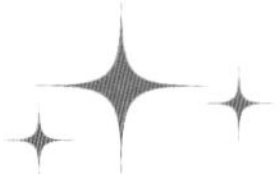

Another Rafaello inspired cake—this time one of the classic, original truffles.
Weighing in grams is essential for the precision and successful result of this recipe. *PRO TIP: For Gluten Free version of this recipe, simply substitute the all-purpose flour with 1:1 Gluten Free flour.

COCONUT CAKE:

285 g (2 1/3 cups) all-purpose flour

2 tsp. baking powder

1/2 tsp. baking soda

1 tsp. salt

170 g (12 Tbsp.) unsalted butter, at room temperature

330 g (1.4 cups) granulated sugar

5 large egg whites, at room temperature

120 g (1/2 cup) sour cream, at room temperature

2 tsp. pure vanilla extract

2 tsp. coconut extract

125 ml (1/2 cup) canned coconut milk, at room temperature

70 g (1 cup) shredded unsweetened coconut

COCONUT ALMOND FILLING:

1 can of sweetened condensed milk

250 g (2 cups) finely chopped roasted unsalted almonds

250 g (3 cups) unsweetened shredded coconut

ALMOND SWISS MERINGUE BUTTERCREAM:

see complete recipe for the original SMBC on page 14, chapter 3. Substitute vanilla extract for almond extract.

GARNISH:

Rafaello truffles

Coconut Cake Directions:

1. Preheat oven to 325 degrees Fahrenheit.
2. Grease/spray four 6-inch cake pans.
3. Whisk the flour, baking powder, baking soda, and salt together. Set them aside.
4. Using a stand mixer fitted with a whisk attachment, beat the butter and sugar together on medium-high speed about 2 minutes or until smooth and creamy. Scrape down the sides and the bottom of the bowl with a silicone spatula as needed.
5. Add in the egg whites until combined, and then add the sour cream, vanilla extract, and coconut extract with the mixer continuously running on low speed. Mix until combined. Mixture will look curdled because of the varying textures and the solid butter combining. Scrape down the sides and the bottom of the bowl as needed.
6. With the mixer still on low speed, slowly add the dry ingredients and the coconut milk. Mix on low speed until combined, and then fold in the shredded coconut with a silicone spatula. Mix it all by hand with the spatula to make sure there are no butter lumps at the bottom of the bowl. The batter will be slightly thick.
7. Pour batter evenly into the cake pans. Weigh them to ensure accuracy, if desired. Bake for around 40–50 minutes or until the cakes are baked through and the inserted toothpick comes out clean and dry. Allow the cakes to cool completely in the pans set on a wire rack upside down. The cakes must be completely cool before frosting and assembling. For best results wrap the cooled cakes in kitchen plastic and either refrigerate or freeze overnight.

Filling Directions:

1. Combine sweetened condensed milk with almonds, coconut, and coconut extract. Fold/mix well.

Assembly:

1. Once the cake layers have cooled in the refrigerator or freezer, trim and torte if needed, resulting in 4 cake layers.
2. Place a thin layer of almond buttercream onto your 8-inch cake board/round. Follow with the placement of a coconut cake layer, lightly pressing to help it adhere to the buttercream and cake round.
3. Pipe a tall ring of almond buttercream along the edges of the cake layer. Smooth out approximately ¼ to half a cup of coconut/almond filling. Repeat with the remaining cake layers and filling.
4. Once the cake has been filled, aligned, and straightened out, place it into the refrigerator for 30 minutes to set. Follow with a crumb coat, and then final perfecting coats of the almond buttercream, refrigerating after every coat.
5. Decorate with piped rosettes and Rafaello truffles.

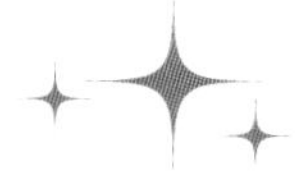

FRENCH ISPAHAN INSPIRED CAKE

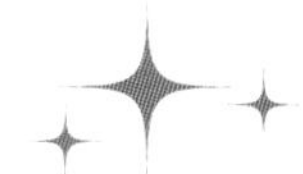

This recipe is inspired by the renowned Pierre Hermes's Ispahan Macarons. After a delightful trip to Paris a few years back, not only I was determined to master some of the French pastries, but I also came back home with such fond memories of these famous Ispahan Macarons. This cake is packed with rose, raspberry, and lychee fruit flavors. It is light, not too sweet, and will magically transport you to the streets of Paris on the fly. Just close your eyes and enjoy a slice of this cake with a cup of tea or coffee.

Weighing in grams is essential for the precision and successful result of this recipe. *PRO TIP: For Gluten Free version of this recipe, simply substitute the all-purpose flour with 1:1 Gluten Free flour.

ALMOND CHIFFON CAKE:

200 g almond paste (store bought, or make your own with recipe below)

4 large eggs, separated, at room temperature

15 g granulated sugar

40 g all-purpose flour

2 g baking powder

30 g unsalted butter, melted and cooled

Pinch of salt

ALMOND PASTE:

100 g blanched almonds

100 g powdered sugar

30 g egg whites

LYCHEE JELLY LAYER:

400 g lychees (fresh or in syrup)

50 g granulated sugar (if using fresh fruit or unsweetened compote)

8 g gelatin powder

20 g cold water

SYRUP:

Lychee syrup from can or cooked lychee

RASPBERRY JELLY LAYER:

400 g fresh or frozen raspberries

80g granulated sugar

8 g gelatin powder

20 g cold water

ROSE MOUSSE LAYER:

3 g gelatin powder

15 g rose water

2 egg yolks

65 g granulated sugar

50 g water

10 edible rose buds

175 g heavy cream (+10 g rose water)

One vanilla bean

RASPBERRY BUTTERCREAM:

add a few drops of purple food coloring gel and 3 tablespoons of powdered freeze-dried raspberries to the French Silk Buttercream recipe on page 15, Chapter 2.

GARNISH:

Fresh or freeze-dried raspberries

Lychee fruit

Edible rose buds and petals

Almond Chiffon Cake Directions:

1. Preheat the oven to 325 degrees Fahrenheit.
2. For almond paste: pulverize the almonds in a food processor. Add the sugar and pulse again until they are evenly combined. Add the egg whites and pulse until a paste has formed.
3. Place the almond paste in the bowl of your mixer together with the yolks and whip them for about 5 minutes until pale and thick.
4. In a separate bowl whip the whites with the salt until stiff peaks have formed.
5. Add the butter to the yolks and gently mix it in.
6. Add half of the whites and gently incorporate them into the batter.
7. Fold in the flour and baking powder.
8. Add the rest of the whites and gently fold them in.
9. Pour the batter into two 6-inch greased pans and bake for about 15–20 minutes. They should spring back when lightly pressed with a finger.
10. Let cakes cool completely before using. For best results wrap the cooled cake layers in kitchen plastic and refrigerate or freeze overnight.

Lychee Jelly Layer Directions:

1. Puree the fruits in a food processor. Place the puree and sugar in a pan on medium heat and boil until all sugar is dissolved.
2. If using fresh fruit, place about 150 ml water and the sugar in a pan and bring to a boil. Add the fruits and allow to simmer for 10 minutes.
3. In the meantime, sprinkle the gelatin over cold water and allow it to bloom for 5 minutes. Mix bloomed gelatin into the hot puree.
4. Pour the jelly in a pan that is the same size as your cake layers and put it in the freezer to set. You can line the pan with aluminum foil or plastic to ease the removal.
5. Reserve the syrup from the can or from boiling the fruits.

Raspberry Jelly Layer Directions:

1. Puree raspberries in a food processor. Place the puree and sugar in a pan on medium heat and boil until all sugar is dissolved.
2. Bloom gelatin powder in cold water for 5 minutes. Mix bloomed gelatin into raspberry puree.
3. Pour the jelly in a pan that is the same size as your cake layers and put it in the freezer to set. You can line the pan with aluminum foil or plastic foil to ease the removal.

Rose Mousse Layer Directions:

1. Place the water, sugar, rose buds and vanilla bean in a pan, cover it and bring to a boil over medium high heat. When it boils, uncover it, lower the heat, and let it cook till you measure 238 degrees Fahrenheit on your sugar thermometer.
2. In the meantime bloom the gelatin in rose water for 5 minutes.
3. Whisk the egg yolks until they become light and fluffy.
4. Place the bloomed gelatin into the microwave for 10–15 seconds to melt.
5. Once the sugar syrup reaches 238 degrees Fahrenheit, remove the bean and the buds, and slowly pour the syrup over the yolks while whisking. You can scrape the bean later into the mousse. Next, pour the melted gelatin over the yolks and continue mixing until the mixture increases in volume, thickens, and cools.

6. Whip the heavy cream in a stand mixer fitted with a whisk attachment till you get soft peaks.
7. Gently fold the whipped cream into the yolk's mixture.

Assembly:

1. Place your cake ring or spring form on a baking sheet lined with parchment paper. Fit the first cake layer inside the ring and brush some lychee syrup over it.
2. Spread 2 tablespoons of mousse over it. It will act as glue between the cake and the jelly. Place the lychee jelly over that and then spread another 2 tablespoons of mousse over that.
3. Place the second cake layer on top, brush it with syrup, spread 1 tablespoons of mousse over it, then place the raspberry jelly on top. Then, pipe all the remaining mousse and level it.
4. Place the cake in the freezer for 6–8 hours.
5. Once the cake has fully set in the freezer, remove it from the ring or spring form and place/align it onto your cake round/board.
6. Follow it with a crumb coat and final perfecting coats of the purple raspberry buttercream, refrigerating after every coat.
7. Decorate with simple piped drop flowers, fresh or freeze-dried raspberries, lychee fruit, and edible rose buds and petals.
8. It is easiest to cut this cake using a sharp knife dipped in hot water

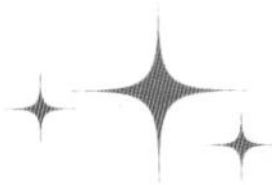

PASSIONFRUIT MANGO MOUSSE CAKE

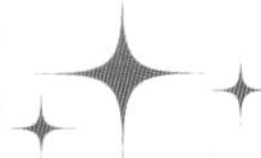

This is one of the first cakes that I made back in the day. The light, not too sweet exotic flavors of passionfruit and mango will have you and your guests asking for seconds.

Weighing in grams is essential for the precision and successful result of this recipe.

PASSIONFRUIT AND MANGO MOUSSES:

500 ml (2 cups) cold heavy cream

112 g (1 cup) powdered sugar

1 tsp. lemon juice (fresh or bottled) or pure lemon extract

2 Tbsp. gelatin powder

8 Tbsp. cold water

200 g passionfruit puree, fresh or frozen

200 g fresh or frozen mango puree

MIRROR GLAZE:

8 Tbsp. glucose syrup

135 g (2/3 cup) granulated sugar

4 Tbsp. cold water

10–12 g gelatin powder + 4 Tbsp. cold water

6 Tbsp. condensed milk

150 g (1 cup) white chocolate

food coloring gels

GARNISH:

Fresh or freeze-dried edible flowers

Slices of passionfruit and mango

Passionfruit and Mango Mousses Directions:

1. Separately puree the passionfruit and mango (if using fresh/frozen whole fruit) and set aside.
2. Add cold heavy cream, powdered sugar and lemon juice into the stand mixer bowl and whip on high speed with the whisk attachment until it doubles in volume and achieves stiff peaks. Separate into 2 bowls.
3. Meanwhile, bloom gelatin with cold water for 5 minutes. Put 1 tablespoon gelatin powder + 4 tablespoon cold water in 2 separate small bowls.
4. Melt bloomed gelatin in the microwave for 10–20 seconds, fold half into the mango puree and the other half into the passionfruit puree.
5. Fold the mango/gelatin mixture into one half of the freshly whipped cream, and passionfruit/gelatin mixture into the other half of the whipped cream.
6. Add each of the mousses into separate piping bags.
7. If using a spring form or a short silicone round mold line the bottom and sides of the form with parchment paper or acetate.
8. Fill half of your silicone mold or spring form with mango mousse, freeze for 15 minutes.
9. Remove mold/form from freezer and fill the other half of the mold/form with passionfruit mousse. Freeze for 15 minutes. Once the mousse cake has fully set in the freezer for at least 8 hours remove the mousse cake from the silicone mold or the spring form and set it on the flipped upside-down wide cup, with a glass or bowl set over the tray that will catch the pouring mirror glaze. This can later be collected, reserved, recolored, and reused.

Mirror Glaze Directions:

1. Place white chocolate into large heatproof bowl and set aside.
2. Bloom gelatin by placing the gelatin powder and cold water into small bowl, mixing well and setting aside for at least 5 minutes.
3. Place glucose syrup, sugar, water into a small pot and bring it to a boil on medium heat. Remove from heat and mix in bloomed gelatin. As soon as the gelatin has melted—pour this mixture over the white chocolate, but do not mix. Let it sit for 5 minutes.
4. Whisk well until the white chocolate fully melts.
5. Separate into three measuring cups. Color one with pink, the other with orange, and the third with yellow food coloring gels.
6. Let cool off until you read 37 degrees Fahrenheit on the sugar thermometer before pouring it over the frozen mousse cake.

Assembly:

1. Pour the mirror glaze over the frozen mousse cake, making sure that the entire top surface and the sides are covered. Wait for 10–15 minutes for the mirror glaze to fully drip down before removing excess drips from the bottom of the mousse cake, using a wet knife or offset spatula.
2. Dampen your hands with water and remove the mirror glazed mousse cake from the cup/bowl and set it over the cake board or serving platter.
3. Decorate with fresh or freeze-dried edible flowers, slices of passionfruit and mango, or just leave it as is if desired.

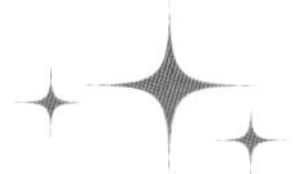

TRIPLE CHOCOLATE MOUSSE CAKE

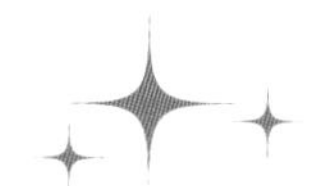

Three chocolates, three decadent mousses. This recipe can be used for making even individual mousse cups, or mini entremets. I highly recommend using a good quality chocolate, such as Lindt, Ghirardelli or Callebaut Chocolate for the best, most flavorful results.

Weighing in grams is essential for the precision and successful result of this recipe. Measurements in cups are not included, nor recommended.

WHITE CHOCOLATE MOUSSE:

6 g gelatin powder

36 g cold water

1 egg

40 g granulated sugar

70 g whole milk

70 g white chocolate

180 g heavy cream

MILK CHOCOLATE MOUSSE:

6 g gelatin powder

36 g cold water

1 egg

40 g granulated sugar

70 g whole milk

70 g milk chocolate

180 g heavy cream

DARK CHOCOLATE MOUSSE:

6 g gelatin powder

36 g cold water

1 egg

40 g granulated sugar

70 g whole milk

70 g dark chocolate

180 g heavy cream

White Chocolate Mousse Directions:

1. Sprinkle gelatin powder over cold water and allow it to bloom for at least 5 minutes.
2. Add the egg and sugar into the bowl of the stand mixer fitted with a whisk attachment and whisk on high speed for 5 minutes. Continue until the mixture turns lighter in color, doubles in volume, and becomes airy and fluffy.
3. Reduce the mixer speed to low and add milk. Once the milk has incorporated, add the mixture to a medium sized pot and bring to a boil over medium heat, constantly whisking with a hand whisk.
4. Once the milk/egg/sugar mixture starts boiling, remove it from the heat and add the bloomed gelatin, whisk to combine.
5. Add white chocolate and then whisk to combine. Set it aside to cool to room temperature.
6. Whip the heavy cream to stiff peaks on high speed in a stand mixer fitted with a whisk attachment.
7. Fold in cooled white chocolate mixture.
8. Using an 8-inch spring form or silicone mold lined with acetate sheet or parchment paper, pour in the white chocolate mousse, filling 1/3 of the form. Freeze for 15 minutes while you are preparing the milk chocolate mousse.

Milk Chocolate Mousse Directions:

1. Sprinkle gelatin powder over cold water and allow it to bloom for at least 5 minutes.
2. Add egg and sugar into the bowl of the stand mixer fitted with a whisk attachment and whisk on high speed for 5 minutes. Continue until the mixture turns lighter in color, doubles in volume, and becomes airy and fluffy.
3. Reduce the mixer speed to low and add milk. Once the milk has incorporated, add the mixture to a medium sized pot and bring to a boil over medium heat, constantly whisking it with a hand whisk.
4. Once the milk/egg/sugar mixture starts boiling, remove it from the heat and add the bloomed gelatin and whisk to combine.
5. Add milk chocolate and then whisk to combine. Set it aside to cool to room temperature.
6. Whip the heavy cream to stiff peaks on high speed in a stand mixer fitted with a whisk attachment.
7. Fold in the cooled milk chocolate mixture.
8. Pour the milk chocolate mousse over the set white chocolate mousse. Freeze it for 15 minutes while you prepare the dark chocolate mousse.

Dark Chocolate Mousse Directions:

1. Sprinkle gelatin powder over cold water and allow it to bloom for at least 5 minutes.
2. Add egg and sugar into the bowl of the stand mixer fitted with a whisk attachment and whisk on high speed for 5 minutes. Continue until the mixture turns lighter in color, doubles in volume, and becomes airy and fluffy.
3. Reduce the mixer speed to low and add milk. Once the milk has incorporated, add the mixture to a medium sized pot and bring to a boil over medium heat, constantly whisking with a hand whisk.
4. Once the milk/egg/sugar mixture starts boiling, remove it from the heat and add the bloomed gelatin, whisk to combine.
5. Add dark chocolate and then whisk to combine. Set aside to cool to room temperature.
6. Whip the heavy cream to stiff peaks on high speed in a stand mixer fitted with a whisk attachment.
7. Fold in cooled dark chocolate mixture.
8. Pour the dark chocolate mousse over a set milk chocolate mousse and freeze for at least 4 hours or overnight.
9. Once the mousse cake has set, remove it from the spring form/silicone mold, place it on a cake board/serving platter and enjoy.

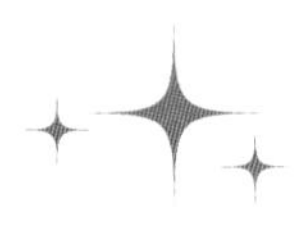

RASPBERRY DARK CHOCOLATE MOUSSE CAKE

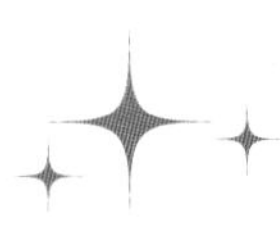

Weighing in grams is essential for the precision and successful result of this recipe. Measurements in cups are not included, nor recommended.

DARK CHOCOLATE MOUSSE:

6 g gelatin powder

36 g cold water

1 egg

40 g granulated sugar

70 g whole milk

70 g dark chocolate

180 g heavy cream

RASPBERRY MOUSSE:

8 g gelatin powder

40 g cold water

40 g granulated sugar

150 g heavy cream, cold

70 g white chocolate

150 g raspberry puree

20 g unsalted butter

100 g fresh or frozen whole raspberries

Dark Chocolate Mousse Directions:

1. Sprinkle gelatin powder over cold water and allow it to bloom for at least 5 minutes.
2. Add the egg and sugar into the bowl of the stand mixer fitted with a whisk attachment and whisk on high speed for 5 minutes. Continue until the mixture turns lighter in color, doubles in volume, and becomes airy and fluffy.
3. Reduce the mixer speed to low and add the milk. Once the milk has incorporated, add the mixture to a medium sized pot and bring it to a boil over medium heat, constantly whisking it with a hand whisk.
4. Once the milk/egg/sugar mixture starts boiling, remove it from the heat and add the bloomed gelatin, whisk to combine.
5. Add the dark chocolate and then whisk to combine. Set it aside to cool to room temperature.
6. Whip the heavy cream to stiff peaks on high speed in a stand mixer fitted with a whisk attachment.
7. Fold in the cooled dark chocolate mixture.

Raspberry Mousse Directions:

1. Place the raspberry puree and the sugar into a medium sized pot, stir, and bring to a boil over medium heat until all the sugar has dissolved. Remove from heat and allow the mixture to come to room temperature.
2. Meanwhile, sprinkle the gelatin over cold water and allow it to bloom for at least 5 minutes.
3. Combine the white chocolate and butter in the microwave safe bowl. Microwave for 10–20 seconds intervals, stirring in between each session until all the chocolate and butter have melted and combined.
4. Melt the bloomed gelatin in the microwave for 10–15 seconds.
5. Combine the gelatin, raspberry, and white chocolate mixtures together, mix well with a whisk until combined and smooth.
6. Whip the heavy cream in a stand mixer fitted with a whisk attachment until there are soft peaks and combine it with the raspberry/chocolate mixture and the whole raspberries. Mix it well with a silicone spatula.

Assembly:

1. Line an 8-inch spring form or a silicone round mold with an acetate wrap, kitchen plastic, or parchment paper. Place it on a flat large portable surface, such as a cutting board (for the ease of transferring to the freezer and for preventing any mousse escaping from the pan/mold.)
2. Pour the raspberry mousse and then place the form/mold into the freezer for 10–15 minutes. Then pour the chocolate mousse over the raspberry mousse and freeze for at least 5–6 hours.
3. Decorate as desired or leave it as is.

ORANGE CAKE WITH CRANBERRY CONFITURE AND MILK CHOCOLATE CREAM

THE HOLIDAY SEASON EXTRAVAGANZA

Oh, this cake has a special meaning. Are you ready? My maiden name means "Cranberry" in our language and all 11 years in school almost no one called me by my first name, but rather by my nickname "klyukvachka", which is like a daring name for "cranberry". Cranberries played another part in our household during my childhood: whenever anyone was sick, my mom made us eat fresh cranberries with honey. Even though they are pretty tart on their own, one had to go through this "sacrifice" as cranberries are packed with vitamin C, antioxidants, and according to my mom—were a magical cure for any disease. Thankfully, I've always loved Cranberries. To my enjoyment—immigrating to America also meant introduction to Thanksgiving, turkey, and cranberry sauce (which I absolutely love). With Holidays quickly approaching, and my nostalgic association of it with oranges, cranberries, and chocolate, I am sharing with you one of my Thanksgiving and Christmas staples: a delightful, citrusy, sweet, and tart fluffy cake that I hope will make an appearance at several of your celebrations.

Weighing in grams is essential for the precision and successful result of this recipe. *PRO TIP: For Gluten Free version of this recipe, simply substitute the all-purpose flour with 1:1 Gluten Free flour.

ORANGE CHIFFON CAKE:

4 eggs, at room temperature

250 g (1 cup + 3 Tbsp.) granulated sugar

1 tsp. vanilla

55 g (4 Tbsp.) vegetable oil

125 g (½ cup) milk

270 g (2 ⅛ cups) all-purpose flour

1 tsp. baking powder

Zest of 1 orange

40 g (3 Tbsp.) hot water

CRANBERRY CONFITURE:

250 g (1 cup) fresh or frozen cranberries

80 g (5 Tbsp.) granulated sugar

1 tsp. gelatin powder

4 Tbsp. cold water

MILK CHOCOLATE MOUSSE CREAM:

6 g gelatin powder

36 g cold water

1 egg

40 g granulated sugar

70 g whole milk

70 g milk chocolate

180 g heavy cream

CAKE SOAK:

80 grams of orange juice

40 grams of sugar

ORANGE BUTTERCREAM:

Add a few drops of orange food coloring gel and 3 tablespoons of powdered freeze-dried oranges (optional) to the Swiss Meringue Buttercream recipe on page 14, Chapter 2.

GARNISH:

Sparkling Cranberries

Tangerines or Orange Slices

Orange Chiffon Cake Directions:

1. Whip the eggs and sugar in a stand mixer fitted with a whisk attachment for 5–8 minutes on high speed until light and fluffy.
2. Combine oil, milk, and zest in a separate bowl and slowly add it to the whipped eggs while the mixer is still going on low speed.
3. Sift the dry ingredients together and set them to one side.
4. Add the dry ingredients to the mixer, alternating with hot water. You want to have four parts dry, and three parts wet.
5. Split the batter into two 8-inch greased cake pans.
6. Bake at 328 degrees Fahrenheit for 40–60 minutes.
7. Once cooked, flip the cakes onto a cooling rack, remove the parchment paper, and allow to cool completely for at least an hour.

Cranberry Confiture Directions:

1. Drizzle the gelatin powder over water and allow it to bloom for at least 5 minutes.
2. Puree the cranberries in a food processor or blender. Strain to remove any large pieces if there are any. Combine with the sugar in a medium sized pot and place it on low heat. Boil for 2 minutes and then remove it from the heat.
3. Melt the bloomed gelatin and combine it with the cranberry sauce. Let them cool to room temperature before use.

Milk Chocolate Mousse Cream Directions:

1. Sprinkle gelatin powder over cold water and allow it to bloom for at least 5 minutes.
2. Add the egg and sugar into the bowl of the stand mixer fitted with a whisk attachment and whisk on high speed for 5 minutes until the mixture turns lighter in color, doubles in volume, and becomes airy and fluffy.
3. Reduce the mixer speed to low and add the milk. Once the milk has incorporated, add the mixture to a medium sized pot and bring it to a boil over medium heat, constantly whisking with a hand whisk.
4. Once the milk/egg/sugar mixture starts boiling, remove it from the heat and add the bloomed gelatin, whisk to combine.
5. Add the milk chocolate and then whisk to combine. Set aside to cool to room temperature.
6. Whip the heavy cream to stiff peaks on high speed in a stand mixer fitted with a whisk attachment.
7. Fold in the cooled milk chocolate mixture.

Assembly:

1. Once the cake layers have cooled in the refrigerator or freezer, trim and torte if needed, resulting in 4 cake layers.
2. Place a thin layer of orange buttercream onto your 8-inch cake board/round. Follow with the placement of an orange chiffon cake layer drizzled with 1-3 tablespoons of cake soak, lightly pressing to help it adhere to the buttercream and cake round.
3. Pipe a tall ring of orange buttercream along the edges of the cake layer. Smooth out approximately ¼ to half a cup of milk chocolate mousse cream, placing and smoothing 2-3 tablespoons of cranberry confiture over. Repeat with the remaining cake layers and filling.
4. Once the cake has been filled, aligned, and straightened out, place it into the refrigerator for 30 minutes or freezer for 15 minutes to set. Follow with a crumb coat, and then final perfecting coats of the orange buttercream, refrigerating or freezing after each.
5. Decorate with piped buttercream rosettes/drop flowers, tangerines or orange slices, and sparkling cranberries.

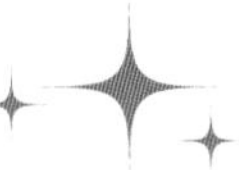

SIGNATURE VANILLA VERY BERRY CAKE

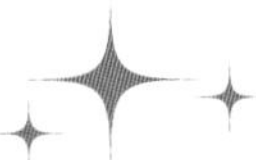

Berries and Cream—that can be a second name for this cake. It is the summeriest, the creamiest, the berriest cake you have ever tried. I serve it all year long and for any occasions. It contains classic vanilla chiffon cake layers, my signature "ice-cream" cream, and loads of fresh berries.

Weighing in grams is essential for the precision and successful result of this recipe. *PRO TIP: For Gluten Free version of this recipe, simply substitute the all-purpose flour with 1:1 Gluten Free flour.

VANILLA CHIFFON CAKE:

135 g (2/3 cup) unsalted butter, at room temperature

450 g (2 ½ cups) granulated sugar

115 g (8 ½ Tbsp.) vegetable oil

6 eggs, at room temperature

500 g (3 cups + 2 Tbsp.) all-purpose flour

250 ml (1 cup) whole milk, at room temperature

1 tsp. baking powder

1 tsp. salt

1 Tbsp. clear vanilla (clear is preferred, but not required)

"ICE-CREAM" CREAM:

450 g (2 cups) mascarpone cheese, cold

1 Tbsp. sour cream or Greek yogurt, cold

250 ml (1 cup) whipping cream (liquid), cold

240 g (2 cups) powdered sugar

1 tsp. of vanilla extract (clear or powdered vanilla sugar preferred)

FILLING AND GARNISH:

Fresh, washed and dried berries (strawberries, raspberries, blueberries, blackberries)

Optional: red and black currants, mint leaves, edible microgreens

Vanilla Chiffon Cake Directions:

1. Preheat oven to 328 degrees Fahrenheit.
2. Mix the oil, butter, and sugar together with a whisk attachment in a stand mixer for 5 minutes until light and fluffy.
3. Add eggs one at a time, scraping down the bowl in between.
4. Sift the dry ingredient together and set them to one side. Combine the wet ingredients together.
5. Add the dry ingredients to the mixer, alternating with the wet. You want to have 4 parts dry, 3 parts wet.
6. Split the batter into two 8-inch greased cake pans.
7. Bake at 328 degrees Fahrenheit for 40–60 minutes.
8. Once cooked, flip the cakes onto a cooling rack, remove the parchment paper, and allow them to cool completely for at least 1 hour.

"Ice-cream" Cream Directions:

1. Add all ingredients into your mixer bowl and mix with a whisk attachment on low speed, slowly increasing to high speed for about 5 minutes until the cream has thickened and doubled in volume. Be careful to not overmix.

Assembly:

1. Place a small amount of cream onto your cake round/drum or serving platter, followed by the first layer of vanilla cake with the smoothest/flattest side down. Place 1 -1 /2 cups of cream, smooth it out with off-set spatula, add sliced berries, and cover with the second cake layer. Place the filled cake into the refrigerator for 30 minutes.
2. After the cake has cooled and settled in refrigerator, smooth out the top and sides with the remaining cream, keeping a semi-naked rustic look by allowing some cake layers to show.
3. Decorate the top with desired berries, mint leaves, edible micro-greens and flowers.

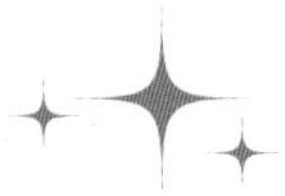

CREAMY OREO CAKE

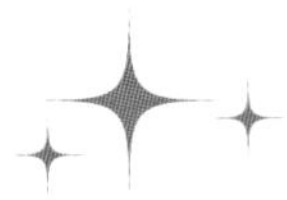

This is for all my Oreo loving friends. My kids would be on the top of that list—words cannot describe how much all three of them love Oreo cookies. I originally developed this recipe per my kids' request. It has been improved and enhanced through the years.

Weighing in grams is essential for the precision and successful result of this recipe. *PRO TIP: For Gluten Free version of this recipe, simply substitute the all-purpose flour with 1:1 Gluten Free flour.

OREO CAKE:

6 eggs, at room temperature

300 g (1 ½ cups) granulated sugar

80 g (6 Tbsp.) vegetable oil

125 ml (½ cup) whole milk

300 g (2 cups) all-purpose flour

1 tsp. salt

1 tsp. baking powder

10 Oreo cookies, roughly crushed in chunks

CAKE SOAK:

35 g (⅛ cup) heavy cream

35 g (⅛ cup) milk

35 g (⅓ cup) sugar

CREAM CHEESE OREO CREAM:

450 g (1 ¾ cups) cream cheese, at room temperature

125 ml (½ cup) heavy cream

50 g (½ cup) powdered sugar

10 Oreo cookies (for this recipe I used limited edition holiday Oreos)

BUTTERCREAM:

Swiss Meringue Buttercream, page 14, Chapter 2, split in half: plain/white and 10 powdered Oreo cookies mixed into the other.

GARNISH:

Oreo cookies

Oreo Cake Directions:

1. Pre-heat oven to 325 degrees Fahrenheit.
2. In the bowl of a stand mixer fitted with a whisk attachment, whip eggs and sugar on high speed for 5-8 minutes.
3. Reduce the mixer speed to low and add milk and oil.
4. Sift together flour, salt, and baking powder. Slowly add these dry ingredients to the wet while the mixer is still mixing on low speed.
5. Remove the bowl from the mixer and fold in crushed Oreo cookies with silicone spatula.
6. Fill your prepared/greased 6-inch baking pans with the batter. Bake on the middle rack at 325 degrees Fahrenheit for 40-45 min until an inserted toothpick comes out dry and clean.
7. Once the cakes have baked, flip them upside down on the cooling rack with the baking pans still intact. Once the cakes/pans have cooled to room temperature, wrap them in kitchen plastic/cling film and either refrigerate them or freeze before use.

Cake Soak Directions:

1. Combine all the ingredients in a small pot; bring to a just starting to boil stage while continuously mixing on low heat. Take off the heat and allow to cool to room temperature.

Cream Cheese Oreo Cream Directions:

1. Powder the Oreo cookies.
2. Combine cream cheese, heavy cream, powdered sugar, and whip mixture on high speed until it forms stiff peaks.
3. Reduce the mixer speed to low and add in the Oreo powder then whip on high speed until it is all combined.

Assembly:

1. Place a small layer of white buttercream onto an 8-inch cake board/round. Follow it with a cake layer, a ring of white buttercream around the edges of the cake layer, and then the Oreo cream in the center. Repeat with the remaining cake layers and filling.
2. Once the cake has been filled, aligned, and straightened out, place it into the refrigerator for 30 minutes to set.
3. Follow with a crumb coat and the final perfecting coats of white buttercream, refrigerating after every coat.
4. Once the final coat of white buttercream has been smoothed and perfected use a striped comb to create the stripe gaps.
5. Place the cake into the freezer for 20-30 minutes. Meanwhile, fit a piping bag with a half inch piping tip (Wilton 10 or 11) and fill with Oreo buttercream.
6. Remove the chilled cake from the freezer and fill the stripe gaps with Oreo buttercream. Overfilling the gaps is a key here—at the end it will all come together to clean, perfect stripes.
7. Once the stripe gaps have been filled with the Oreo buttercream, you can start smoothing/scraping the sides of the cake with your bench scraper or cake scraper. It will take lots of turns and many scrapes to get to your desired result.
8. When you are happy with the cleanliness of your stripes place the cake into the freezer for 15 minutes. Then warm up your bench or cake scraper with hot water and finish cleaning up your stripes.
9. Finish decorating with piped rosettes alternating with Oreo cookies along the top edge of the cake.

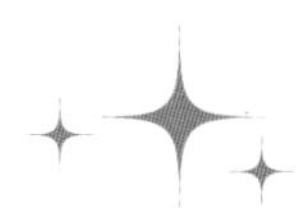

STRAWBERRY-LICIOUS CAKE

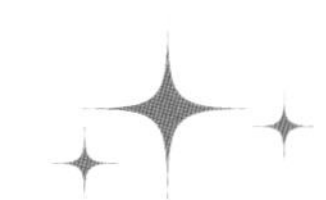

This delightful, refreshing cake is packed with strawberry flavor. If you are like me and might make this cake year-round without access to fresh strawberries—using frozen strawberries will lead you to the same delicious result.

Weighing in grams is essential for the precision and successful result of this recipe. *PRO TIP: For Gluten Free version of this recipe, simply substitute the all-purpose flour with 1:1 Gluten Free flour.

STRAWBERRY JAM:

400 g (3 cups) fresh diced strawberries

6 Tbsp. maple syrup or sugar

1 Tbsp. cornstarch

2 Tbsp. water

2 Tbsp. lemon juice (fresh or bottled)

1 tsp. lemon zest

STRAWBERRY CAKE:

135 g (2/3 cup) unsalted butter, at room temperature

450 g (2 ½ cups) granulated sugar

115 g (8 ½ Tbsp.) vegetable oil

5 eggs, at room temperature

500 g (3 cups + 2 Tbsp.) all-purpose flour

250 ml (1 cup) whole milk, at room temperature

1 tsp. baking powder

1 tsp. salt

1 Tbsp. clear vanilla (clear is preferred, but not required)

half a batch of strawberry jam

STRAWBERRY BUTTERCREAM:

1 batch of my Swiss Meringue Buttercream, page 14, chapter 2

125 g powdered freeze-dried strawberries

CHOCOLATE GANACHE:

90 g white chocolate

30 g cold heavy cream (well shaken)

GARNISH:

Drop flowers

Fresh strawberries

Edible flowers

Strawberry Jam Directions:

1. Combine diced strawberries and maple syrup or sugar in medium sized saucepan and bring it to a boil over medium heat.
2. Cook/reduce it for 4–6 minutes, occasionally stirring.
3. Add cornstarch dissolved in water and lemon juice and bring it back to a boil.
4. Cook for an additional 3 minutes, continuously stirring.
5. Remove from heat, transfer it to a heatproof container, and allow it to come to room temperature.

Strawberry Cake Directions:

1. Preheat oven to 325 degrees Fahrenheit.
2. Beat oil, butter, and sugar with a whisk attachment on high speed for about 5 min until light and fluffy.
3. Add eggs, one at a time, while continuously whisking on low speed, scraping down the bowl in between.
4. Sift the dry ingredients together and set them aside.
5. Combine the wet ingredients together.
6. Add the dry ingredients to the mixer, alternating with the wet.
7. Fold in the half batch of strawberry jam. Optional: fold in flour dusted 1/2 cup of diced fresh strawberries.
8. Split the batter into the prepared cake pans.
9. Bake for 40–50 min for 6-inch cake pans, until an inserted toothpick comes out clean/dry with just a few crumbles on it. Do not open your oven during the first 30 minutes of your baking; otherwise, your cakes may not rise. Baking times may vary based on the strength of your oven and the quality/size of your baking pans.

Chocolate Ganache Directions:

1. Place your chocolate and heavy cream in a microwave safe container, microwave in 30 seconds intervals, vigorously mixing the ganache in between heating sessions.
2. Once all the chocolate has melted and combined well with the heavy cream—mix in a few drops of pink food coloring gel, and set it aside to cool to room temperature, occasionally whisking. Drips can be applied with a teaspoon or a drip bottle.

Assembly:

1. Place a small layer of strawberry buttercream onto your 8-inch cake board/round. Follow it with a cake layer, smooth out a thin layer of strawberry buttercream over the cake layer and then pipe a ring of strawberry buttercream around the edges of the cake layer. This will ensure that you trap the strawberry jam to keep it from escaping/oozing out from between the cake layers.
2. Place or pipe the strawberry jam in the center inside the piped buttercream ring. Optional: add fresh strawberry chunks if desired. Repeat with the remaining cake layers and the filling.
3. Once the cake has been filled, aligned, and straightened out, place it into the refrigerator for 30 minutes to set. Follow it with a crumb coat and then the final perfecting coats of strawberry buttercream, refrigerating after every coat.
4. Once the final buttercream coat has been perfected and smoothed, place the cake into the freezer for 15–30 minutes. Meanwhile prepare the drip and let it cool to room temperature. It shouldn't be hotter than 37–40 degrees Celsius/100–104 degrees Fahrenheit.
5. Test the drip for consistency on the back of the cake or a clean cup/glass. Apply the drip along the edges and top of the cake. Place the cake into the freezer for 10–15 minutes so the drips can set and harden.
6. Decorate with piped buttercream rosettes, drop flowers, fresh strawberries, and edible flowers if desired.

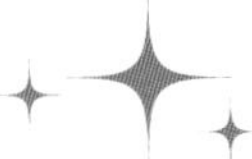

PISTACHIO RASPBERRY MILK CAKE

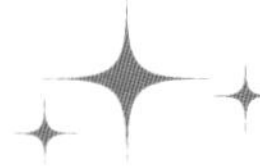

Pistachio and raspberry are one of the pastry worlds' absolute classics of flavor combinations, and my own personal favorite. This warming, nutty, sweet and tangy cake will not only please the eye with its natural gorgeous colors, but also will delight with its taste, texture, and become that perfect pair for coffee and tea times, celebrations, and special occasions, and "just because" all year round.

Weighing in grams is essential for the precision and successful result of this recipe. *PRO TIP: For Gluten Free version of this recipe, simply substitute the all-purpose flour with 1:1 Gluten Free flour.

PISTACHIO CHIFFON CAKE:

300 g (1 3/4 cups + 2 Tbsp.) all-purpose flour

300 g (1 1/2 cups) granulated sugar

2 1/2 tsp. baking powder

1/2 tsp. salt

175 g (3/4 cup, 1 1/2 sticks) unsalted butter, at room temperature

6 large egg yolks, at room temperature (save whites for buttercream)

3 Tbsp. pistachio paste (store-bought or make yourself by processing pistachios in food processor until it reaches the consistency of paste)

250 ml (1 cup) whole milk, at room temperature

1 1/2 tsp. pure vanilla extract

RASPBERRY JAM:

250 g (1 1/2 cups) fresh or frozen raspberries (washed and dried)

3 tsp. granulated sugar

1 tsp. lemon juice (fresh or bottled)

RASPBERRY MILK BUTTERCREAM:

300 g egg whites (from approximately 9 eggs), at room temperature

150 g (2/3 cup) caster/superfine sugar

398 g (1 can) of sweetened condensed milk

1/2 tsp. salt

1 tsp. pure vanilla extract

1/2 cups freeze-dried raspberries, finely ground into powder

GARNISH:

Fresh or freeze-dried raspberries

Pistachios

Pistachio Cake Directions:

1. Preheat oven to 325 degrees Fahrenheit and spray cake pans with baking spray.
2. In a stand mixer fitted with a whisk attachment and mixer bowl, whisk together the wet ingredients and set them aside.
3. In a separate bowl, sift and whisk together all the dry ingredients, add the butter and half of the wet ingredients, and mix well until they are combined.
4. Add the remaining wet ingredients, mixing well until all the wet ingredients are incorporated.
5. Divide batter evenly between four prepared 6-inch cake pans and bake approximately 35–45 minutes or until a toothpick inserted into the center comes out clean.
6. Cool in pans on a wire rack upside down. Wrap each cake layer in kitchen plastic/cling film and refrigerate them overnight before filling the cake.

Raspberry Jam Directions:

1. Mix the raspberries, sugar and lemon juice in a medium saucepan. Cook on medium-high heat until it thickens, stirring constantly. Cover and freeze for 10–15 minutes until it cools.

"Raspberry Milk" Buttercream Frosting Directions:

1. Place the egg whites and sugar into the bowl of a stand mixer, whisk until combined
2. Place bowl over a hot water bath and whisk constantly until the mixture is no longer grainy to the touch (approx. 3 mins or until your sugar thermometer reaches 65 degrees Fahrenheit).
3. Place bowl in your stand mixer and whisk on high speed until the meringue is stiff and cooled, approximately 8–10 minutes. The bowl should no longer be warm to the touch.
4. Switch to a paddle attachment. Slowly add the cubed butter and vanilla and mix until smooth.
5. Add the sweetened condensed milk in 3 steps, allowing each addition to fully incorporate while continuously whisking on low speed.
6. Add the powdered freeze-dried raspberries. Whip on low speed until smooth for about 2 minutes.

Assembly:

1. Place a small layer of raspberry buttercream onto your 8-inch cake board/round. Follow it with a pistachio cake layer, smooth out a thin layer of raspberry buttercream over the cake layer and then pipe a ring of raspberry buttercream around the edges of the cake layer. This will ensure that you trap the raspberry jam and keep it from escaping/oozing out from between the cake layers.
2. Place or pipe the raspberry jam in the center inside the piped buttercream ring. Optional: add fresh raspberries if desired.
3. Repeat with the remaining cake layers and the filling. Once the cake has been filled, aligned, and straightened out, place it into the refrigerator for 30 minutes or freezer for 15–20 minutes to set.
4. Decorate the top and bottom borders of the cake with fresh or freeze-dried raspberries and pistachios.

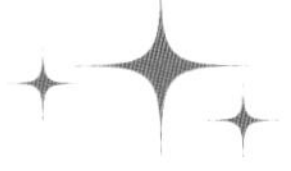

SUGAR-FREE SOUR CHERRY LEMON CAKE

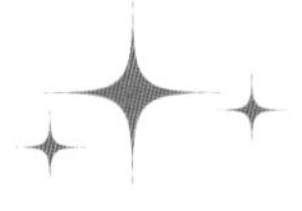

Meet my new citrusy, cherry sugar-free cake. I am so delighted to share this sugar-free version of one of my signature cakes—it has that perfect sweet lemon and sour cherry punch, minus the refined sugar. Enjoy!

Weighing in grams is essential for the precision and successful result of this recipe. *PRO TIP: For Gluten Free version of this recipe, simply substitute the all-purpose flour with 1:1 Gluten Free flour.

SOUR CHERRY LEMON CAKE:

135 g (2/3 cup) unsalted butter, at room temperature

250 g (1 1/4 cup) monk sugar

115 g (8 1/2 Tbsp.) vegetable oil

5 eggs, at room temperature

500 g (3 cups + 2 Tbsp.) all-purpose flour

250 ml (1 cup) whole milk, at room temperature

1 tsp. baking powder

1 tsp. salt

1 Tbsp. lemon extract

140 g (1 cup) fresh or frozen pitted sour cherries, rolled in flour

SUGAR-FREE SILKY BUTTERCREAM:

Sugar-Free Silky Buttercream recipe on page 11, Chapter 2, substitute vanilla extract for lemon extract

50 g sour cherry puree

GARNISH:

Maraschino cherries

Sour Cherry Lemon Cake Directions:

1. Preheat the oven to 325 degrees Fahrenheit
2. Place oil, butter, and monk sugar into the stand mixer bowl. Fit the mixer with a whisk attachment and beat the above ingredients together for 5 minutes on high speed until the mixture becomes light and fluffy.
3. Reduce the mixer speed to low and add the eggs one at a time, scraping down the bowl in between each addition.
4. Sift the dry ingredients together and set them aside.
5. Combine the wet ingredients in a separate bowl and set them aside.
6. While the mixer is still running on low speed, add the dry ingredients to the mixer, alternating with the wet. You want to have 3 parts dry, and 2 parts wet ingredients.
7. Fold in the floured sour cherries by hand using a silicone spatula.
8. Fill your prepared (greased or lined) 6-inch baking pans with the batter, 2/3 full.
9. Bake at 325 degrees Fahrenheit for 40–50 min until an inserted toothpick comes out dry and clean. Do not open your oven for the first 30 minutes, or your cakes may not rise and bake properly.
10. Cool on a wire rack, upside down, with the cake pans intact until the cakes chill to room temperature. Wrap them into plastic wrap/ cling film and either refrigerate them for a few hours before use or freeze overnight to ease out the cake filling, decorating, stacking process. Trim and torte the cold cake layers if needed before filling/assembling the cake.

Sour Cherry Sugar-Free Buttercream Directions:

1. Use the Sugar-Free Silky Buttercream recipe from page 11, Chapter 2. Substitute vanilla extract for lemon.
2. Puree the pitted fresh or frozen sour cherries, add to the sugar-free buttercream, and whip on low speed in a stand mixer fitted with the whisk attachment.
3. Add 3–5 drops of burgundy or dark pink food coloring gel if desired.

Assembly:

1. Place a thin layer of lemon/cherry buttercream onto your 8-inch cake board/round. Follow it with a placement of a cherry cake layer, lightly pressing to help it adhere to the buttercream and cake round. Smooth out approximately ¼ to half a cup of buttercream. Repeat with the remaining cake layers and frosting.
2. Once the cake has been filled, aligned, and straightened out, place it into the refrigerator for 30 minutes to set. Follow it with a crumb coat and then the final perfecting coats of the buttercream, refrigerating after every coat.
3. Decorate as desired. I chose to use 8B piping tip by Wilton, adding "drop kisses" and "sea-shell" piping along the bottom and side of the cake, as well as the top border, then garnishing with maraschino cherries.

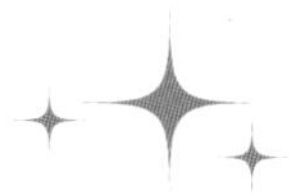

RAINBOW MARBLE PARTY CAKE

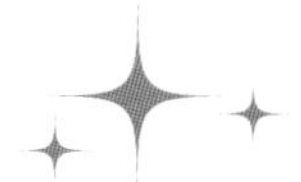

Ah, just look at those cheerful, colorful rainbow marble cake layers. In this recipe not only will I teach you how to let the colored cake layers bake perfectly, preserving the color and preventing browning, but also, I will share all my tricks on how to achieve those perfect, crisp, clean stripes. Get your rainbow popcorn and sparkles ready—time to party.

Weighing in grams is essential for the precision and successful result of this recipe. *PRO TIP: For Gluten Free version of this recipe, simply substitute the all-purpose flour with 1:1 Gluten Free flour.

RAINBOW MARBLE CAKE:

135 g (2/3 cup) unsalted butter, at room temperature

450 g (2 ½ cups) granulated sugar

115 g (8 ½ Tbsp.) vegetable oil

egg whites from 5 eggs, at room temperature

500 g (3 cups + 2 Tbsp.) all-purpose flour

250 ml (1 cup) whole milk, at room temperature

1 tsp. baking powder

1 tsp. salt

1 Tbsp. clear vanilla (clear is preferred, but not required)

Gel Food Colors (Neon gel colors work best for this recipe and are my favorite to use.)

SWISS MERINGUE BUTTERCREAM:

Swiss Meringue Buttercream, page 14 Chapter 2

GARNISH:

Colorful Popcorn

Sparkling Sugars or Sprinkles

Rainbow Marble Cake Directions:

1. Preheat oven to 310 degrees Fahrenheit.
2. Beat oil, butter, and sugar together in the bowl of a stand mixer fitted with a whisk attachment for 5 minutes until it turns light and fluffy.
3. Add the egg whites about one tablespoon at a time, scraping down the bowl in between.
4. Sift the dry ingredient together and set them aside.
5. Combine the wet ingredients together, set them aside.
6. Add the dry ingredients to the mixer, alternating with the wet. You want to have 3 parts dry, two parts wet.
7. Split batter into 5–7 (depending on number of colors desired) bowls and add 3–4 drops of desired food coloring gels. I used neon food coloring gels by Chefmaster: neon pink, neon purple, neon green, neon blue, neon yellow, and neon orange for both the cake layers and for the stripes.
8. Prepare four 6-inch cake pans. Use approximately 350–400 g of batter per cake pan. Pans must be filled 2/3 of the way. Pour about 2 tablespoons of each color of the batter into cake pans, alternating the colors, and then swirl with a toothpick or skewer.
9. Bake at 310 degrees Fahrenheit for 45–55 minutes until an inserted toothpick comes out clean and dry. The key to success of baking the colored batter is the "low and slow" method: you bake on a lower temperature for a longer time, to preserve the color and prevent browning.
10. Once baked, flip the cakes onto a cooling rack, and allow to cool completely for at least 1 hour, then wrap in cling film and refrigerate or freeze overnight (preferred).

White and Rainbow Buttercream Directions:

1. Make one batch of my Swiss Meringue Buttercream, according to the recipe on page 14, Chapter 2.
2. Put half of the buttercream into a separate bowl and let it remain uncolored—this is the white buttercream that you will use for filling and frosting the cake.
3. Split the other half of the buttercream into 6 separate small bowls and add 3–4 drops of desired food coloring gels. I used neon food coloring gels by Chefmaster: neon pink, neon purple, neon green, neon blue, neon yellow, and neon orange.

Assembly:

1. Place a small layer of white buttercream onto your 8-inch cake board/round. Follow it with a cake layer and a thin layer of white buttercream. I used approximately ¼ of a cup. Repeat this with the remaining cake layers and filling.
2. Once the cake has been filled, aligned, and straightened out, place it into the refrigerator for 30 minutes to set. Follow it with a crumb coat and the final perfecting coats of white buttercream, refrigerating after every coat.
3. Once the final coat of white buttercream has been smoothed and perfected use a striped comb to create the stripe gaps. Place the cake into the freezer for 20–30 minutes.
4. Meanwhile, fit 6 piping bags with the colored buttercreams, one piping bag for each color. Cut approximately a half an inch opening in each of the piping bags.
5. Remove the chilled cake from the freezer and fill the stripe gaps with colored buttercream. Here I filled in the following order: purple, blue, pink, orange, yellow, green, purple. Overfilling the gaps is the key here—at the end it will all come together to clean, perfect stripes.
6. Once the stripe gaps have been filled with the colored buttercreams, you can start smoothing/scraping the sides of the cake with your bench scraper or cake scraper. It will take lots of turns and many scrapes to get to your desired results. When you are happy with the cleanliness of your stripes place the cake into the freezer for 15 minutes. Then warm up your bench or cake scraper with hot water, wipe it dry, and finish cleaning up your stripes. Make sure to wipe the scraper with paper towel after every turn so your scraper is always clean before starting the new scraping turn.
7. Finish decorating with sparkling sugars, sprinkles, and popcorn.

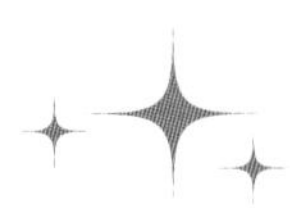

PUMPKIN SPICE LATTE INSPIRED CAKE

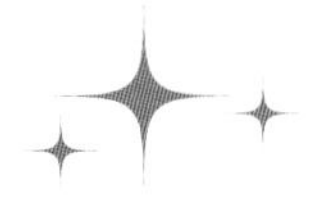

Yep, this cake is inspired by Starbuck's pumpkin spice latte, also known as PSL. I wait for the end of August every year since it was launched just to stand in long drive through or walk in pick-up lines to get my first PSL of the fall season. This cake is flavorful, warm, and cozy, as comforting as the famous fancy latte itself. It pairs extremely well with falling leaves, knitted sweaters and scarfs.

Weighing in grams is essential for the precision and successful result of this recipe. *PRO TIP: For Gluten Free version of this recipe, simply substitute the all-purpose flour with 1:1 Gluten Free flour.

PUMPKIN SPICE CAKE:

400 g (2 ½ cups) all-purpose flour

3 tsp. baking powder

1/5 tsp. pumpkin pie spice

1tsp. salt

113 g (½ cup, 1 stick) unsalted butter melted, cooled

110 g (½ cup) vegetable oil

270 g (1 ⅓ cup) granulated sugar

245 g (1 cup, packed) light-brown sugar, packed

500 g pumpkin puree (2 cups) (can be substituted with apple sauce, sweet potato puree, or squash puree)

4 large eggs, at room temperature

CAFE LATTE BUTTERCREAM FILLING:

300 g (from 9 eggs) of fresh or carton egg whites, at room temperature

250 g (1 ¼ cups) caster/superfine sugar

565 g (2 ½ cups, 5 sticks) of unsalted butter, at room temperature

4 ½ Tbsp. instant coffee dissolved in 3 tsp. hot water OR 4 tsp. of expresso, cooled

HOMEMADE DULCE DE LECHE:

See page 10, Chapter 2 for directions on how to make it

EGGLESS CONDENSED MILK BUTTERCREAM::

See page 8, Chapter 2 for full recipe

GARNISH:

Edible gold dusts

Edible gold leaf

Pumpkin Cake Directions:

1. Preheat oven to 325 degrees Fahrenheit and spray three 6-inch cake pans with baking spray.
2. In a medium bowl, sift and whisk together the flour, pumpkin pie spice, baking powder, and salt.
3. In a large bowl, whisk together the sugars, melted butter, oil, pumpkin puree, and eggs.
4. Add dry ingredients to the wet and mix them until combined.
5. Divide batter evenly between prepared cake pans and bake for approximately 35–40 minutes until a toothpick inserted into the center comes out clean.
6. Cool in pans on a wire rack upside down. Wrap the cooled cakes into kitchen plastic and refrigerate or freeze overnight.

Cafe Latte Buttercream Directions:

1. Place the egg whites and sugar into the bowl of a stand mixer, whisk until combined.
2. Place the bowl over a double boiler hot water bath on the stove and whisk constantly until the mixture is no longer grainy to the touch (approx. 3 mins or until your sugar thermometer reaches 150 degrees Fahrenheit/65 degrees Celsius).
3. Place bowl on your stand mixer and whisk on high speed for approximately 8–10 minutes or until the meringue is stiff and cooled and the bowl is no longer warm to the touch.
4. Reduce the mixer speed to low. Slowly add the butter, one tablespoon at a time, and mix until smooth.
5. Add the espresso/coffee mixture. Whip it until smooth on high speed, for approximately 8 minutes. Reduce the speed to low and allow it to beat for a few more minutes for a smooth, bubble-free result.

Assembly:

1. Place a small layer of Condensed Milk Buttercream onto your 8-inch cake board/round. Follow it with a cake layer, lightly pressing on it to help it adhere to the cake round. Smooth out a thin layer and then pipe a ring of Café Latte Buttercream around the edges of the cake layer, and the Dulce de Leche in the center. Follow it with another thin layer of café latter buttercream. Repeat with the remaining cake layers and filling. Once the cake has been filled, aligned, and straightened out, place it into the refrigerator for 30 minutes to set. Follow it with a crumb coat and then the final perfecting coats of Condensed Milk Buttercream, refrigerating after every coat.
2. Decorate by piping mini pumpkins with the piping tip #8B by Wilton, leaves piped with the Wilton's piping tip #70, edible gold dusts, and edible gold leaf.

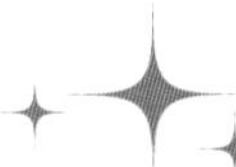

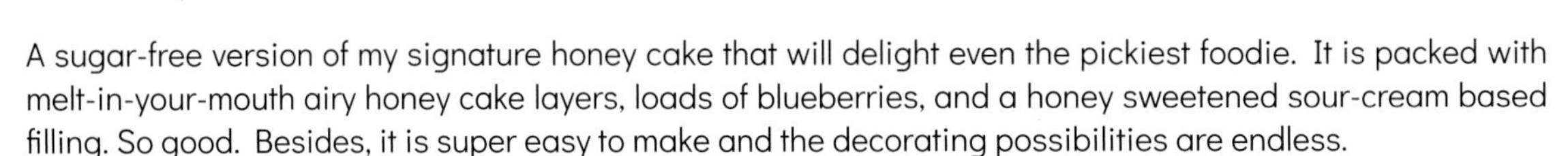

SUGAR-FREE HONEY BLUEBERRY CAKE

A sugar-free version of my signature honey cake that will delight even the pickiest foodie. It is packed with melt-in-your-mouth airy honey cake layers, loads of blueberries, and a honey sweetened sour-cream based filling. So good. Besides, it is super easy to make and the decorating possibilities are endless.

Weighing in grams is essential for precision and a successful result of this recipe. *PRO TIP: For Gluten Free version of this recipe, simply substitute the all-purpose flour with 1:1 Gluten Free flour.

SUGAR-FREE HONEY CAKE:

270 g (2 ⅛ cups) all-purpose flour

Pinch of salt

340 g (1 cup) honey

3 large eggs, at room temperature

2 tsp. baking soda

1 Tbsp. vinegar

GARNISH:

Fresh or frozen blueberries

BLUEBERRY HONEY CREAM:

5 g (1 ½ tsp.) gelatin powder or agar powder

30 g (6 tsp.) cold water

120 g (½ cup) cream cheese, at room temperature

170 g (½ cup) honey

250 ml (1 cup) heavy cream, cold

250 g (1 cup) sour cream, cold

300 g (2 cups) pureed fresh or frozen blueberries

Blueberry Honey Cream Directions:

1. Sprinkle the gelatin over cold water, mix to combine well and allow it to bloom for 5 minutes.
2. In the bowl of a stand mixer fitted with a whisk attachment, whip the cream cheese and honey on high speed until all is well combined.
3. Melt the bloomed gelatin in microwave for 10–15 seconds, add to the cream cheese/honey mixture and allow it to whip on low speed.
4. In a separate bowl, whip the cold heavy cream to soft peaks. Using silicone spatula fold it into the cream cheese/honey mixture. Add cold sour cream and pureed blueberries.
5. Refrigerate for at least 60 minutes while you are preparing/baking the honey cakes.

Sugar-Free Honey Cake Directions:

1. Preheat the oven to 350 degrees Fahrenheit.
2. Sift together the flour and salt, set it aside.
3. Add the eggs to the bowl of a stand mixer fitted with a whisk attachment and whip on high speed for approximately 5 minutes until they double in volume and become lighter in color.
4. Reduce the mixer speed to low, add honey, and gradually increase the speed of the mixer to medium-high. Whip on medium-high speed for 6–8 minutes.
5. Lower the mixer speed to low. Combine the soda and vinegar and add it to the honey mixture.
6. Switch to the paddle attachment, and gradually add the dry ingredients while the mixer is still mixing on low speed. Mix until they all combine to a smooth batter.
7. Fill the greased Wilton's 8-inch easy layer baking pans with the honey batter, approximately to a quarter of an inch thickness. Alternatively, you may bake the thin honey cake layer in sheet pans, cutting out the 8-inch rounds once they cool off.
8. Bake at 350 degrees Fahrenheit for 6–8 minutes on the middle rack till the honey cakes turn to a rich amber color.
9. Allow the baked cakes to fully cool off before removing them from the easy layers or baking sheet.
10. If baking in sheet pans and cutting out the 8-inch rounds save the scraps and pulverize in the processor to a fine powder for further decorating steps.

Assembly:

1. Smooth a thin layer of the honey filling on a 10-inch cake round. Place the first honey cake layer and lightly press it, allowing it to adhere.
2. Follow it by smoothing a thin layer (approximately 80 grams) of the honey cream over the cake, and then add 1 to 2 tablespoons of hulled blueberries. Repeat this with the remaining cake and filling.
3. Place the filled cake into the refrigerator for 30 minutes. Meanwhile, pulverize the honey cake scraps to fine powder.
4. Once the cake has cooled off, smooth out the remaining cream cheese filling over the top and sides of the cake, using an offset spatula or cake scraper. Follow by pressing in the powdered honey cake scraps.
5. Decorate as desired: fresh or frozen blueberries, a honey drip, honeycomb, or edible florals.

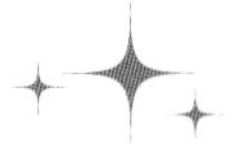

MY LOVE FOR MACARONS IS ENDLESS AND INDESCRIBABLE. There is just something so special about these "troublemakers", these finicky cookies. Besides being irresistibly delicious, they are so photogenic, so beautiful. Every small dessert is so cute, right? Especially macarons. When made correctly, when all the results are delivered, when all the points are hit—they give such a sense of gratitude, satisfaction, and pride. Macarons certainly are not for the faint of heart—they test our patience; they keep us humble. If you have made macarons even once—you surely know what I am talking about.

If you have never made them, I am glad that you are holding my book right now. I am honored that my recipes will give you that first experience and possibly—if you will carefully follow my recipe, tips, and tricks, to the T—you will succeed with your first try. If for any reason you do not, please don't give up. Ever. Even your grocery store may be at fault—what if they sold you super old eggs? Do not ever blame yourself if your macarons do not turn out hitting all the check marks on the list and promise me to CAREFULLY follow my recipe.

I am starting this special chapter of this magical book with my new macaron recipe and method. It took me years to develop it, test it for all food coloring brands, all colors, all baking sheets, all baking mats, and even many different ovens. Oh yes, I did. I did bake at families' houses, friends' houses, and commercial kitchens. Just in case, I tested many different brands of eggs, almond flours, powdered sugars, and even mixers. I can proudly, as loudly as possible, happily scream from the top of my lungs that this Macaron Recipe is IT! It will work for any weather conditions, for any baking sheets/trays, for any silicone baking mats, for any country, any brand of the ingredients. I highly recommend baking your macaron shells on silicone baking mats versus parchment paper for the best, ultimate, perfect results.

This new Macaron Shell recipe is the base for the following 18 recipes, unless noted otherwise, such as chocolate, coffee, brown sugar, Earl Grey, and raspberry macaron recipes.

*NOTE: Weighing in grams is essential for the precision and successful result of macaron making. Measurements in cups are not included, nor recommended in any of the following macaron recipes.

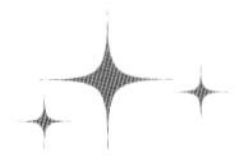

CHAPTER 5

Magical Macaron Universe

19 SUREFIRE RECIPES, INCLUDING MY REUSE REDUCE MACARON SHELLS RECIPE INVENTION

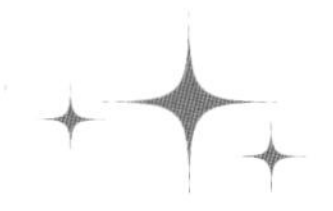

SASHA'S NEW NO REST MACARON SHELLS RECIPE

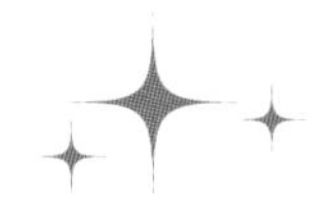

The Base for almost all following 20 recipes.

INGREDIENTS:

125 g egg whites, at room temperature

125 g granulated sugar

6 g egg white powder

132 g powdered sugar

132 g almond flour (not almond meal)

Directions:

1. To be done the night before: separate your egg whites from the egg yolks and leave the covered egg whites on the counter overnight to age. This is one of the best tricks and leads to perfectly whipped stiff peaks that are essential to the success of baked, full macaron shells.
2. Preheat oven to standard, non-convectional, bake setting of 350 degrees Fahrenheit.
3. Add/weigh granulated sugar and egg white powder in a heatproof container or measuring cup. Whisk until it is all combined. Line a baking pan with a sheet of parchment paper and drizzle the sugar mixture over it, spreading evenly, making sure it's not too thin. Lift the edges of the parchment paper on all sides evening out the sugar mixture edges to spread it evenly. Place on the middle rack of the oven and heat for 5 minutes.
4. Add the egg whites into a grease-free, clean, dry stand mixer bowl (wipe with a vinegar or lemon juice-soaked paper towel ahead of time). Mix on low speed until the egg whites start forming bubbles, gradually increasing the speed to medium-low. Once your egg whites start foaming up increase the speed to medium and mix until they become frothy, forming soft peaks. By this time your sugar and egg white powder has warmed up in the oven. Remove it from the oven, and transfer it to the bowl or cup you used to weigh ingredients. The easiest way to do this is to lift the parchment paper from opposite ends, forming a funnel, and carefully pour the sugar mixture into the cup/bowl. Do not turn off the oven—you need it to be ready for the dry ingredients. Reduce the mixer speed to low and add 1 teaspoon of the sugar/egg white powder mixture right on the egg white area between the whisk and the bowl while mixer is continuously whisking on low speed. Be careful not to throw the sugar mixture onto the whisk. Once all the sugar is added, increase the mixing speed to medium and mix it for approximately 3 minutes. Then increase the mixer speed to high and whip for 3–5 minutes until stiff peaks are achieved.

5. While your meringue is getting to stiff peaks, sift together the powdered sugar and almond flour into a separate clean/dry bowl, discarding any large pieces that do not freely pass through the mesh sifter (shouldn't be more than 1 teaspoon). Whisk well to combine.

6. *NOTE: If your almond flour seems to be "wet", coating the sifter, spread it over the parchment paper/baking sheet and "dry" in the oven that you left heating at 350 degrees Fahrenheit for 5 minutes (some almond flours accessible to consumers in any country are "wet", not dry enough for the use in making the macaron batter). After 5 minutes of "drying", remove the almond flour from the oven and sift together with powdered sugar. Whisk well to combine.

7. Once your meringue is ready remove the bowl from the stand mixer and add the almond/powdered sugar mixture all at once. Fold in the dry ingredients into the meringue with a silicone spatula. Once no dry ingredients are visible, start the macaronage. The goal is to remove the air bubbles from the macaron batter without overmixing, by pressing and turning the macaron batter to the side of your bowl. Every 3 turns check it for readiness. Your batter is ready when it freely and slowly flows from your spatula as a thick ribbon, and fully flattens in 30 seconds. Another test is to try drawing the number 8 with the batter slowly flowing from your spatula onto the bowl without breaking. The batter should not be runny—if it is, you have overmixed it.

8. Pre-heat your oven to 320 degrees Fahrenheit again (the oven needs 10 to 20 minutes to come to the right temperature) along with an additional baking sheet on middle rack—baking on doubled baking sheets prevents uneven/lopsided macarons. Add your macaron batter to a piping bag fitted with 0.5 cm round piping tip. Pipe macarons onto a silicone macaron mat placed onto your second oven tray/sheet. I do not recommend using parchment paper as it does not hold the shapes of macarons, nor does it create flat unbroken bottoms. However, if you do not have silicone baking mats yet it's okay to use parchment paper. Holding your piping bag perpendicular to the baking mat, slowly pipe the macaron batter into a one-inch diameter disc, releasing it with a wiping motion. Tap your baking sheet/tray with the piped macaron shells on the counter a few times. Use a toothpick to pop any air bubbles that might appear on the surface of the piped macarons. You do not need to rest these macarons and can place them into the oven immediately (can you believe this?). However, if resting your piped macaron shells is inevitable or preferred, you may do so by resting them for 30 to 40 minutes until the batter forms a skin/doesn't stick and loses some of its shine—results will be the same. Place the baking pan with the silicone mat/parchment paper and piped macaron shells into the oven's middle rack on top of the preheated separate baking sheet. Close the oven and bake for 20–25 minutes, turning the baking tray around halfway after first 10 minutes of baking. Macarons are fully baked when if lightly touched they do not feel wiggly or flimsy. Allow baked macarons to fully cool off before taking them off your macaron mats/parchment.

Pro Tip:

1. If your oven is hot/strong and your white macarons typically "brown" during the baking, place a domed aluminum foil over the white macarons after 10–15 minutes of baking. You may also try baking the white macarons with the following setting: preheat the oven to 350 degrees Fahrenheit, place piped white macaron shells into the oven and immediately reduce the heat to 300 degrees Fahrenheit. Then bake for 25–27 minutes, also covering with foil halfway through baking.

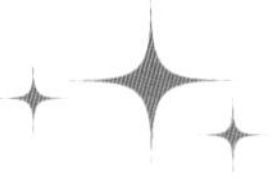

PISTACHIO RASPBERRY MACARONS

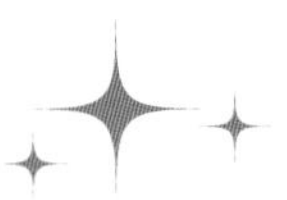

MACARON SHELLS:

Use my New Macaron Recipe at the beginning of this chapter on page 110.

PISTACHIO GANACHE:

220 g heavy cream, cold

100 g high quality white chocolate

20 g pistachio paste

40 g unsalted butter, at room temperature

FILLING:

Freeze-dried, frozen, or fresh raspberries

GARNISH:

Powdered freeze-dried raspberries (optional)

Macaron Shells Directions:

1. Use my New Macaron Recipe from page 110. Once the macronage has been completed, prepare the piping bag fitted with your 10 or 11 piping tips. Using a food safe brush and the inside of the piping bag, draw two opposite lines with avocado or green food coloring gels and two lines of pink or burgundy food coloring gel in between the green ones.

2. Fill the piping bag with the macaron batter and pipe the macaron shells as advised in main/base recipe. Not required/optional: rest/dry the piped macaron shells for 30–40 minutes before baking.

Pistachio Ganache Directions:

1. Heat the heavy cream to just about boiling point and pour over the white chocolate. Mix well with the silicone spatula.

2. Add the pistachio paste and whip on low speed with a hand mixer or emerging blender. Allow it to cool to room temperature.

3. Add the butter and whip again. Cover it with a kitchen plastic/cling film fully touching the surface of the ganache. Place it into the refrigerator for at least 8 hours.

4. Once the ganache sets in the refrigerator, whip it again with the hand mixer or emerging blender, for about 1 minute. Make sure not to overmix.

Assembly:

1. Fit the piping bag with a large round tip, such as 1A or 2A by Wilton, and the pistachio ganache. Pipe "Hershey kisses" like dollops of the pistachio ganache on each half of the pre-matched macaron shells. Place a slice of freeze-dried, frozen, or fresh raspberry in the center. Then cover it with the matching half of the macaron shell, pressing lightly. Optionally you may dust the macarons with powdered freeze-dried raspberries.

2. Refrigerate the filled macarons for at least 24 hours for the shells to absorb the filling. Macarons taste their best after 24 hours of refrigeration, followed by warming up to room temperature for at least 30 minutes before consumption.

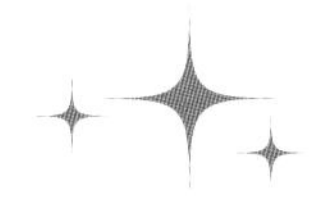

DARK CHOCOLATE ORANGE MACARONS

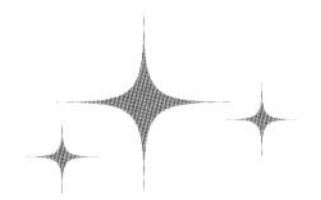

MACARON SHELLS:

Use my New Macaron Recipe at the beginning of this chapter on page 110.

3–6 drops of orange flavoring or freeze-dried orange

DARK CHOCOLATE ORANGE GANACHE:

40 g high quality dark chocolate

170 g heavy cream

1 tsp. of orange zest

GARNISH:

White meringue kisses

Powdered freeze-dried oranges

Raspberries

Macaron Shells Directions:

1. Use my New Macaron Recipe from page 110. Add 3–6 drops of orange food coloring gel (or more, if desired) and orange flavoring or 3 g of powdered freeze-dried orange to the egg whites at the same time when adding the sugar/egg white powder mixture.
2. Once the macaronage has been completed, prepare the piping bag fitted with your 10 or 11 piping tips. Fill the piping bag with the macaron batter and pipe the macaron shells as advised in the main/base recipe. Not required/optional: rest/dry the piped macaron shells for 30–40 minutes before baking.

Dark Chocolate Orange Ganache Directions:

1. Heat the heavy cream to just about boiling point and pour over the dark chocolate. Mix well with the silicone spatula until the heavy cream and the chocolate combine to form a uniform smooth mixture.
2. Fold in the orange zest with a silicone spatula
3. Cover it with kitchen plastic/cling film fully touching the surface of ganache to prevent any condensation. Place it into the refrigerator for at least 8 hours.
4. Once the ganache sets in the refrigerator, whip it again with the hand mixer or emerging blender, for about 1 minute. Make sure not to overmix.

Assembly:

1. Fit the piping bag with a large round tip, such as 1A or 2A by Wilton, and the dark chocolate orange ganache. Pipe "Hershey kisses" like dollops of the ganache on a half of the pre-matched macaron shells. Place a slice of freeze-dried, frozen, or fresh orange in the center if desired. Cover it with the matching half of the macaron shell, pressing lightly. Optionally you may dust the macarons with powdered freeze-dried raspberries or oranges.
2. Refrigerate the filled macarons for at least 24 hours for the shells to absorb the filling. Macarons taste their best after 24 hours of refrigeration, followed by warming up to room temperature for at least 30 minutes before consumption.

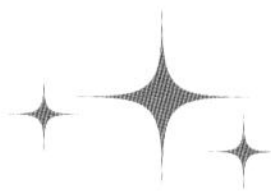

PASSIONFRUIT CHOCOLATE MACARONS

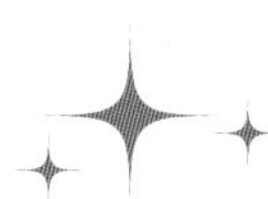

MACARON SHELLS:

Use my New Macaron Recipe at the beginning of this chapter on page 110.

6 g unsweetened cocoa powder

PASSIONFRUIT GANACHE:

60 g fresh or frozen seedless passionfruit puree

55 g heavy cream

10 g butter

125 g high quality white chocolate, chopped

MILK CHOCOLATE ORANGE GANACHE:

40 g high quality milk chocolate

170 g heavy cream

1 tsp. of orange zest

Macaron Shells Directions:

1. Use my New Macaron Recipe from page 110.
2. Add 6 g of unsweetened cocoa powder to the dry ingredients during the second sifting. It is optional to also use a drop or two of brown food coloring to enhance the color of the macarons.
3. Once the macaronage has been completed, prepare the piping bag fitted with your 10 or 11 piping tips. Fill the piping bag with the macaron batter and pipe the macaron shells as advised in the main/base recipe. Not required/optional: Rest/dry the piped macaron shells for 30–40 minutes before baking.

Passionfruit Ganache Directions:

1. Bring the passionfruit puree to a boil. Separately heat the heavy cream in the microwave or on the stove.
2. Pour both liquids over the white chocolate. Mix well with a silicone spatula until all the ingredients have combined to a uniform, smooth finish.
3. Add the cubed butter. Mix well with your silicone spatula until it is combined.
4. Cover it with plastic wrap/cling film—the plastic wrap must be touching and fully covering the surface of the ganache. Refrigerate it for 6–8 hours.
5. Whip the cold ganache with a hand or stand mixer for 1 minute to give it a light, fluffy, strong finish.

Milk Chocolate Ganache Directions:

1. Heat the heavy cream to just about boiling point and pour it over the dark chocolate. Mix well with the silicone spatula until the heavy cream and the chocolate combine to form a uniform smooth mixture.
2. Fold in the orange zest with a silicone spatula
3. Cover it with the kitchen plastic/cling film with it fully touching the surface of ganache to prevent any condensation. Place it into the refrigerator for at least 8 hours.
4. Once the ganache sets in the refrigerator, whip it again with the hand mixer or emerging blender, for about 1 minute. Make sure not to overmix.

Assembly:

1. Fit two piping bags with a small round tip, such as 10 or 11 by Wilton. Add the passionfruit ganache into one bag and the milk chocolate ganache into the other. Pipe the ring of the passionfruit ganache along the outside edge of the halves of the pre-matched macaron shells. Pipe milk chocolate ganache in the center of the passionfruit ganache ring. Cover it with the matching half of the macaron shell, pressing lightly. Optionally you may drizzle your filled macarons with heated/runny passionfruit ganache just as shown on these photos.
2. Refrigerate the filled macarons for at least 24 hours so the shells get to absorb the filling and develop the flavors. Macarons taste their best after 24 hours of refrigeration, followed by warming up to room temperature for at least 30 minutes before consumption

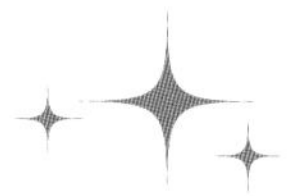

"PEACHES AND ROSES" MACARONS

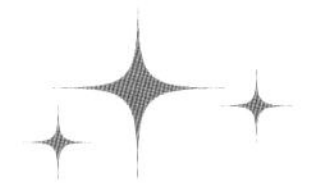

MACARON SHELLS:

Use my New Macaron Recipe at the beginning of this chapter on page 110

½ tsp. Rose water

PEACH AND ROSE JELLY:

200 g fresh hulled, frozen, or canned peaches

1 tsp. gelatin or agar powder

4 Tbsp. cold rose water

PEACH BUTTERCREAM:

Use my Signature Swiss Meringue Buttercream recipe from page 14, Chapter 2

Peach extract

Orange food coloring gel

Macaron Shells Directions:

1. Use my New Macaron Recipe from page 110. Add ½ teaspoon of rose water to macaron batter right before finishing the macronage. Once the macaronage has been completed, separate the batter into 2 separate bowls, and color one with 2–3 drops of pink or rose food coloring and the other with 6–8 drops of same food coloring. This will result in lighter and darker pink macaron batters.
2. Prepare the piping bag fitted with 10 or 11 piping tips. Fill half of the piping bag with light pink macaron batter and the other half with dark pink batter. Pipe the macaron shells as advised in the main/base recipe. Not required/optional: rest/dry the piped macaron shells for 30–40 minutes before baking.

Peach Buttercream Directions:

1. Use my Signature Swiss Meringue Buttercream recipe from page 14, Chapter 2.
2. Make half of the batch if desired, flavoring with peach extract and mixing in 5–10 drops of orange food coloring gel.

Peach and Rose Jelly Directions:

1. Sprinkle the gelatin or agar powder over the rose water and allow it to bloom for 5–10 minutes.
2. Meanwhile, puree the peaches and place into a medium sized bowl over medium heat. Bring to a boil and add the bloomed gelatin or agar. Mix well to combine.
3. Transfer to a heatproof shallow container and refrigerate to set for at least an hour while you are preparing/baking the macaron shells.
4. Using a back of a small piping tip, such as the ones you use for piping macarons (#10 or #11 by Wilton) cut out the discs from the set jelly. These are the centers of our macaron filling.

Assembly:

1. Fit a piping bag with a small round tip, such as 10 or 11 by Wilton, and add the peach buttercream. Pipe a ring of the peach buttercream along the outside edge of the halves of the pre-matched macaron shells. Place the peach/rose jelly disc in the center. Cover it with the matching half of the macaron shell, pressing lightly.
2. Refrigerate the filled macarons for at least 24 hours so the shells get to absorb the filling and develop the flavors. Macarons taste their best after 24 hours of refrigeration, followed by warming up to room temperature for at least 30 minutes before consumption.

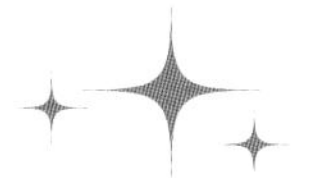

DULCE DE LECHE MACARONS

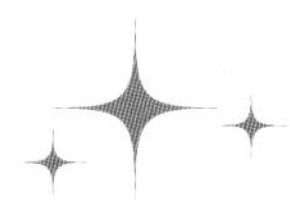

(MADE WITH BROWN SUGAR)

BROWN SUGAR MACARON SHELLS:

125 g egg whites, at room temperature

125 g dark brown sugar

8 g egg white powder

132 g powdered sugar

132 g almond flour (not almond meal)

DARK CHOCOLATE GANACHE:

40 g high quality dark chocolate

170 g heavy cream

DULCE DE LECHE BUTTERCREAM:

226 g (2 sticks) unsalted butter, at room temperature

397 g (1 can) homemade Dulce de Leche, at room temperature

Brown Sugar Macaron Shells Directions:

1. To be done the night before: separate your egg whites from the egg yolks and leave the covered egg whites on the counter overnight, to age. This is one of the best tricks and leads to perfectly whipped stiff peaks that are essential to the success of baked macaron shells.
2. Preheat oven to standard, non-convectional, bake setting of 350 degrees Fahrenheit.
3. Add/weigh the dark brown sugar and egg white powder in a heatproof container or glass measuring cup. Whisk until it is all combined. Line a baking pan with a sheet of parchment paper and drizzle the sugar mixture over it, spreading evenly, making sure it's not too thin. Lift the edges of the parchment paper on all sides evening out the sugar mixture edges to spread it evenly. Place on the middle rack of the oven and heat for 3 minutes.
4. Add the egg whites into a grease-free, clean, dry stand mixer bowl (wipe with a vinegar or lemon juice-soaked paper towel ahead of time). Mix on low speed until the egg whites start forming bubbles, gradually increasing the speed to medium-low. Once your egg whites start foaming up increase speed to medium and mix until they become frothy, forming soft peaks. By this time your brown sugar and egg white powder mixture has warmed up in the oven. Remove it from the oven and transfer it to the used cup or bowl that you weighed ingredients in. The easiest way to do this is to lift the parchment paper from opposite ends, forming a funnel, and carefully pouring the sugar mixture into the cup/bowl. Do not turn off the oven—you need it to be ready for the dry ingredients. Reduce mixer speed to low. Add 1 teaspoon of the brown sugar/egg white powder mixture right on the egg white area between the whisk and the bowl while mixer is continuously whisking it on low speed. Be careful not to throw the sugar mixture onto the whisk. Once all sugar is

added, increase the mixing speed to medium and mix for approximately 3 minutes. Then increase the mixer speed to high and whip for 3–5 minutes until stiff peaks are achieved.

5. While your meringue is getting to stiff peaks, sift together powdered sugar and almond flour into a separate clean/dry bowl. Discard any large pieces that do not freely pass through the mesh sifter (shouldn't be more than 1 teaspoon).

6. Once your meringue is ready—remove the bowl from the stand mixer and add the almond/powdered sugar mixture all at once. Fold in dry ingredients into the meringue with a silicone spatula. Once no dry ingredients are visible, start the macaronage. The goal is to remove the air bubbles from the macaron batter without overmixing. This is achieved by pressing and turning the macaron batter to the side of your bowl. Every 3 turns—check it for readiness. Your batter is fully ready when it freely and slowly flows from your spatula as a thick ribbon, and fully flattens in 30 seconds. Another test is to try drawing the number 8 with the batter slowly flowing from your spatula onto the bowl without breaking. The batter should not be runny. If it is, you have overmixed it.

7. Pre-heat your oven to 320 degrees Fahrenheit again (Any oven needs 10 to 20 minutes to come to the right temperature.) along with an additional baking sheet on middle rack. Baking on doubled baking sheets prevents uneven/ lopsided macarons. Add your macaron batter to a piping bag fitted with 0.5 cm round piping tip. Pipe the macarons onto a silicone macaron mat placed onto your second oven tray/sheet. I do not recommend using parchment paper as it does not hold the shapes of macarons, nor does it give you flat unbroken bottoms. However, if you do not have silicone baking mats yet, it's okay to use parchment paper. Holding your piping bag perpendicular to the baking mat, slowly pipe the macaron batter into a one-inch diameter disc, releasing it with a wiping motion. Tap your baking sheet/tray with the piped macaron shells on the counter a few times. Use a toothpick to pop any air bubbles that might appear on the surface of the piped macarons. Resting these macaron shells is optional—you may bake them immediately or rest for 30 to 40 minutes until the batter forms a skin/doesn't stick and loses some of its shine. Place the baking pan with the silicone mat piped macaron shells into the oven's middle rack on top of the preheated separate baking sheets. Bake for 20–25 minutes. Turn the baking tray around halfway after first 10 minutes of baking. Macarons are fully baked when they do not feel wiggly or flimsy if lightly touched. Allow baked macarons to fully cool off before taking them off your macaron mats.

Dark Chocolate Ganache Directions:

1. Heat the heavy cream to just about boiling point and pour over the dark chocolate. Mix well with the silicone spatula until the heavy cream and the chocolate combine together to a uniform smooth mixture.

2. Cover it with the kitchen plastic/cling film fully touching the surface of the ganache to prevent any condensation. Place it into the refrigerator for at least 8 hours.

3. Once the ganache sets in the refrigerator, whip it again with the hand mixer or emerging blender, for about 1 minute. Make sure not to overmix.

Dulce de Leche Buttercream Directions:

1. In a bowl of a mixer fitted with a whisk attachment, whip the butter for approximately 8 minutes until it has tripled in volume and become light and fluffy. Stop to scrape the bottom of the bowl a few times.

2. Reduce the speed of the mixer to low and add the previously prepared and cooled homemade Dulce de Leche in thirds, whipping for about 8–10 seconds after each addition. Don't forget to scrape the bottom of the bowl after each addition.

Assembly:

1. Fit one piping bag with a small round tip, such as 10 or 11 by Wilton, and add the dark chocolate ganache. Fit another piping bay with a small open star tip, such as #34 by Wilton, and the Dulce de Leche buttercream. Pipe a ring of the ganache along the outside edge of the halves of the pre-matched macaron shells. Pipe a dollop of the Dulce de Leche buttercream in the center. Cover it with the matching half of the macaron shell, pressing lightly.

2. Refrigerate the filled macarons for at least 24 hours so the shells get to absorb the filling and develop the flavors. Macarons taste their best after 24 hours of refrigeration, followed by warming up to room temperature for at least 30 minutes before consumption.

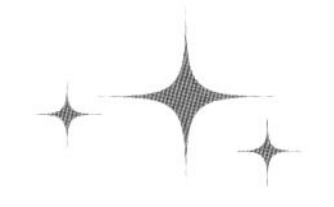

RUBY CHOCOLATE STRAWBERRY MACARONS

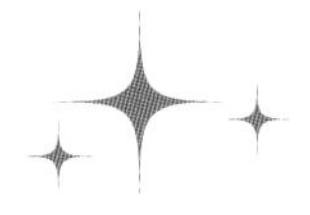

MACARON SHELLS:

Use my New Macaron Recipe at the beginning of this chapter on page 110

8 g unsweetened cocoa powder

RUBY STRAWBERRY GANACHE:

60 g fresh or frozen strawberry puree

55 g heavy cream

125 g high quality ruby chocolate

Macaron Shells Directions:

1. Use the New Macaron Recipe from page 110. Add 8 g of unsweetened cocoa powder to the dry ingredients during the second sifting. Add 4–8 drops of brown food coloring gel to the macaron batter during the macaronage. Once the macaronage has been completed, prepare the piping bag fitted with your 10 or 11 piping tips.
2. Fill the piping bag with the macaron batter and pipe the macaron shells as advised in the main/base recipe. Not required/optional: rest/dry the piped macaron shells for 30–40 minutes before baking.

Ruby Strawberry Ganache Directions:

1. Bring the strawberry puree and heavy cream to a boil.
2. Pour both liquids over the ruby chocolate and let it stand for 1 minute. Mix well with a silicone spatula until all the ingredients have combined to a uniform, smooth finish.
3. Cover it with plastic wrap/cling film—the plastic wrap must be touching and fully covering the surface of the ganache. Refrigerate fit or 6–8 hours.
4. Whip the cold ganache with a hand or stand mixer for 1 minute to give a light, fluffy, and strong finish.

Assembly:

1. Fit a piping bag with a large round piping tip, such as 1A or 2A by Wilton, and add the strawberry ganache. Pipe "Hershey kisses" like dollops in the center of each half of the pre-matched macaron shells. Cover it with the matching half of the macaron shell, pressing lightly.
2. Refrigerate the filled macarons for at least 24 hours so the shells get to absorb the filling and develop the flavors. Macarons taste their best after 24 hours of refrigeration, followed by warming up to room temperature for at least 30 minutes before consumption.

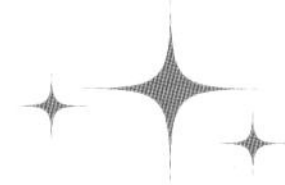

WHIPPED CAFE MOCHA MACARONS

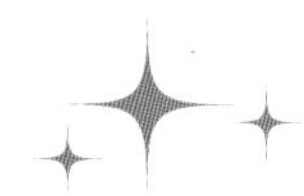

MACARON SHELLS:

Use my New Macaron Recipe at the beginning of this chapter on page 110

8 g powdered instant coffee

WHIPPED WHITE CHOCOLATE COFFEE GANACHE:

100 g high quality white chocolate, chopped

80 g heavy cream

5 g powdered instant coffee

GARNISH:

Coffee beans

White meringue kisses

Macaron Shells Directions:

1. Use the New Macaron Recipe from page 110. Add 8 g of powdered instant coffee to the dry ingredients during the second sifting and 3–5 drops of brown food coloring gel to the macaron batter during the macaronage.
2. Once the macaronage has been completed, prepare the piping bag fitted with your 10 or 11 piping tips. Fill the piping bag with the macaron batter and pipe the macaron shells as advised in the main/base recipe. Not required/optional: rest/dry the piped macaron shells for 30–40 minutes before baking.

Whipped White Chocolate Coffee Ganache Directions:

1. Bring the heavy cream to a boil. Mix in the powdered instant coffee.
2. Pour over the chopped white chocolate and let it stand for 1 minute. Mix well with a silicone spatula until all the ingredients have combined to form a uniform, smooth finish.
3. Cover it with plastic wrap/cling film—the plastic wrap must be touching and fully covering the surface of the ganache. Refrigerate it for 6–8 hours.
4. Whip the cold ganache with a hand or stand mixer for 1 minute to get a light, fluffy, strong finish.

Assembly:

1. Fit the piping bag with an 8B piping tip by Wilton and the whipped coffee ganache. Pipe "Hershey kisses" like dollops in the center of each half of the pre-matched macaron shells. Cover it with the matching half of the macaron shell, pressing lightly.
2. Refrigerate the filled macarons for at least 24 hours so the shells get to absorb the filling and develop the flavors. Macarons taste their best after 24 hours of refrigeration, followed by warming up to room temperature for at least 30 minutes before consumption.

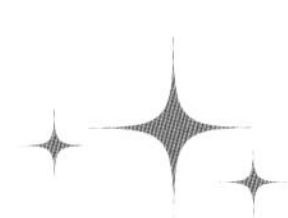

ULTIMATE STRAWBERRY LEMONADE MACARONS

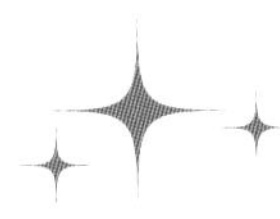

MACARON SHELLS:

Use my New Macaron Recipe at the beginning of this chapter on page 110

LEMON BUTTERCREAM:

226 g (2 sticks) unsalted butter, at room temperature

397 g (1 can) sweetened condensed milk, at room temperature

Zest of 1 lemon

Juice of 1 lemon

STRAWBERRY CREAM:

180 g fresh or frozen strawberries, chopped

80 g sugar

2 egg yolks

30 g cornstarch

85 g unsalted butter, at room temperature

Macaron Shells Directions:

1. Use my New Macaron Recipe from page 110 Once the macaron batter is ready and macaronage has been completed, divide the batter in two separate bowls. Add 3-5 drops of yellow food coloring gel to one bowl, and 3-5 drops of pink food coloring gel to the other. Fold the food coloring gels, pressing the batter in and make sure not to overmix. Stop folding the batters once all the food coloring gel is mixed in.
2. Prepare the piping bag fitted with your number 10 or 11 piping tip. Swipe/add the yellow macaron batter to one side of the piping bag, and the pink macaron batter to the other, and pipe the macaron shells as advised in the main/base recipe. Not required/optional: rest/dry the piped macaron shells for 30-40 minutes before baking.

Lemon Buttercream Directions:

1. In the bowl of a mixer fitted with a whisk attachment, whip the butter for approximately 8 minutes until it has tripled in volume and become light and fluffy. Stop to scrape the bottom of the bowl a few times.
2. Reduce the speed of the mixer to low and add the sweetened condensed milk in thirds, whipping for about 8-10 seconds after each addition. Don't forget to scrape the bottom of the bowl after each addition.
3. While the mixer is running on low speed, add the lemon zest and lemon juice. Allow to whip on low speed for additional 1-2 minutes. Optional: add 3-6 drops of yellow food coloring gel.

Strawberry Cream Directions:

1. Add the strawberries and half of the sugar to the medium sized pan, bring to a boil. Keep boiling on medium heat for about 6-8 minutes.
2. Remove the reduced strawberries from the heat and puree with the emerging blender or in a food processor. Set them aside.
3. Whip the egg yolks, corn starch, and the other half of the sugar till you get a uniform light consistency.
4. While continuously whisking the egg yolk mixture, slowly drizzle into it the strawberry puree.
5. Return this mixture to the medium pot and heat on medium heat, while continuously whisking, until it thickens.
6. Remove the mixture from the heat and transfer to a heatproof container. Cover it with kitchen plastic/cling film—making sure that the plastic is touching the full surface of the cream. Set aside until it cools off to room temperature.
7. Add the cubed butter and whip with a hand or stand mixer for about one minute.

Assembly:

1. Fit two piping bags with small round tips, such as 10 or 11 by Wilton, and add the lemon buttercream to one and the strawberry cream into the other. Pipe a ring of the lemon buttercream along the outside edge of the halves of the pre-matched macaron shells. Pipe a dollop of strawberry cream in the center. Cover it with the matching half of the macaron shell, pressing lightly.
2. Refrigerate the filled macarons for at least 24 hours so the shells get to absorb the filling and develop the flavors. Macarons taste their best after 24 hours of refrigeration, followed by warming up to room temperature for at least 30 minutes before consumption.

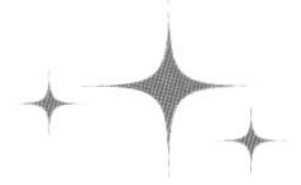

PUMPKIN SPICE LATTE MACARONS

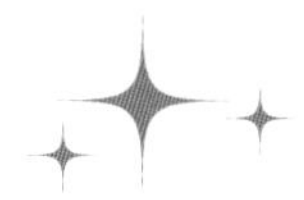

MACARON SHELLS:

Use my New Macaron Recipe at the beginning of this chapter on page 110

PUMPKIN SPICE FILLING:

226 g (2 sticks) unsalted butter, at room temperature

397 g (1 can) homemade Dulce de Leche, at room temperature

¼ tsp. of pumpkin spice

GARNISH:

Edible luster or metallic gold dust

Macaron Shells Directions:

1. Use my New Macaron Recipe from page 110. Add 3–6 drops of pink or burgundy food coloring gel to the macaron batter during the macaronage.
2. Once the macaronage has been completed, prepare the piping bag fitted with your 10 or 11 piping tip and macaron batter. Using my templated double-sided pumpkin/apple baking mat, or a pumpkin printable template under any other silicone mat, pipe the pumpkins as advised in the main/base recipe. Not required/optional: rest/dry the piped macaron shells for 30–40 minutes before baking.

Pumpkin Spice Filling Directions:

1. In the bowl of a mixer fitted with a whisk attachment, whip the butter for approximately 8 minutes until it has tripled in volume and become light and fluffy. Stop to scrape the bottom of the bowl a few times.
2. Reduce the speed of the mixer to low and add the previously prepared and cooled homemade Dulce de Leche in thirds, whipping for about 8–10 seconds after each addition. Don't forget to scrape the bottom of the bowl after each addition.
3. Add the pumpkin spice and whip on low speed for an additional 2–4 minutes.

Assembly:

1. Fill the macarons with the pumpkin spice buttercream. Alternatively, you can dust the grooves and the stem of the pumpkin macarons with edible luster or metallic gold dust.
2. Refrigerate the filled macarons for at least 24 hours so the shells get to absorb the filling and develop the flavors. Macarons taste their best after 24 hours of refrigeration, followed by warming up to room temperature for at least 30 minutes before consumption.

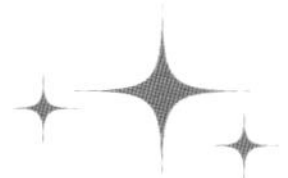

CHRISTMAS MINT MACARONS

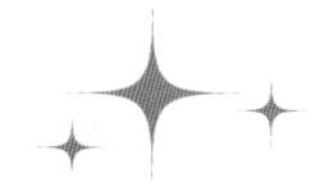

WHITE MACARON SHELLS:

Use my New Macaron Recipe at the beginning of this chapter on page 110

MINT WHITE CHOCOLATE GANACHE:

25 g fresh mint leaves

130 g heavy cream

110 g high quality white chocolate, chopped

GARNISH:

Crushed mints or candy canes

White meringue kisses

---

*Pro Tip:

1. If your oven is hot/strong and your white macarons typically "brown" during the baking, place a domed aluminum foil over the white macarons 10–15 minutes after the start of baking. You may also try baking the white macarons with the following settings: preheat the oven to 350 degrees Fahrenheit, place piped white macaron shells into the oven and immediately reduce the heat to 300 degrees Fahrenheit. Then bake for 25–27 minutes, also covering with foil halfway through baking.

White Macaron Shells Directions:

1. Use my New Macaron Recipe from page 110.

Mint White Chocolate Ganache Directions:

1. Add the heavy cream and the mint leaves to a medium pot. Place it on low heat and bring it to a boil. Remove it from the stove and set aside for 5 minutes.
2. Place the pot back onto the low heat and bring it to a boil one more time. Take it off the heat and pour the heavy cream through the mesh sifter over the chopped white chocolate, catching the mint leaves in the sifter. Set it aside for 5 minutes to rest, and then mix it well with a silicone spatula until all the white chocolate has melted and combined with the mint heavy cream.
3. Cover it with kitchen plastic/cling film making sure that the plastic is fully covering and laying over the surface of the ganache. Place it into the refrigerator for 10–12 hours to set.
4. Once 10–12 hours have passed, whip the cold ganache with a hand or stand mixer for about 1 minute. Make sure not to overmix.

Assembly:

1. Fit the piping bag with 1A or 2A piping tips by Wilton and the whipped mint ganache. Pipe "Hershey kisses" like dollops in the center of each half of the pre-matched macaron shells. Cover it with the other half of the macaron shell, pressing lightly. Roll the centers of the filled/closed macarons in crushed peppermints or candy canes.
2. Refrigerate the filled macarons for at least 24 hours so the shells get to absorb the filling and develop the flavors. Macarons taste their best after 24 hours of refrigeration, followed by warming up to room temperature for at least 30 minutes before consumption.

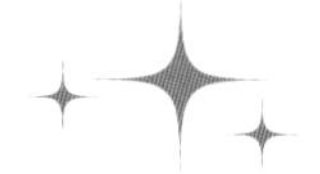

FIG AND HONEY MACARONS

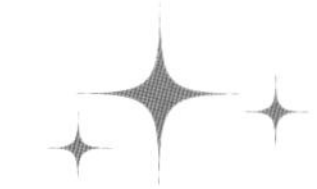

MACARON SHELLS:

Use my New Macaron Recipe at the beginning of this chapter on page 110

FIG GANACHE:

60 g fresh or frozen fig puree, or powdered freeze-dried figs (Amazon)

55 g heavy cream

125 g high quality white chocolate, chopped

FILLING:

Honey

Macaron Shells Directions:

1. Use the New Macaron Recipe from page 110. Once the macaron batter is ready and macaronage has been completed, divide the batter in two separate bowls. Add 3–5 drops of green or neon green food coloring gel to one bowl, and 3–5 drops of purple or neon purple food coloring gel to the other.
2. Fold the food coloring gels, pressing the batter in and making sure not to overmix. Stop folding the batter once all the food coloring gel is mixed in.
3. Prepare the piping bag fitted with a number 10 or 11 piping tip. Swipe/add the green macaron batter to one side of the piping bag, and the purple macaron batter to the other, and pipe macaron shells as advised in the main/base recipe. Not required/optional: rest/dry the piped macaron shells for 30–40 minutes before baking.

Fig Ganache Directions:

1. If using puree: bring the fig puree and the heavy cream to a boil.
2. Pour both liquids over the chopped white chocolate and let it stand for 1 minute. Mix well with a silicone spatula until all the ingredients have combined to a uniform, smooth finish. If using powdered freeze-dried figs instead, add/mix them into the chocolate/heavy cream at this point.
3. Cover it with plastic wrap/cling film. The plastic wrap must be touching and fully covering the surface of the ganache. Refrigerate for 6–8 hours.
4. Whip the cold ganache with a hand or stand mixer for 1 minute to get a light, fluffy, strong finish.

Assembly:

1. Fit a piping bag with a large round piping tip, such as 1A or 2A by Wilton, and add the fig ganache. Pipe "Hershey kisses" like dollops in the center of each half of the pre-matched macaron shells. Add a dollop of honey to the center of piped ganache. Cover it with the matching half of the macaron shell, pressing lightly.
2. Refrigerate the filled macarons for at least 24 hours so the shells get to absorb the filling and develop the flavors. Macarons taste their best after 24 hours of refrigeration, followed by warming up to room temperature for at least 30 minutes before consumption.

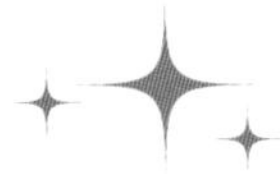

PEAR MINT GANACHE MACARONS

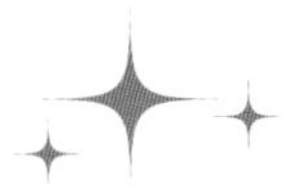

*NOTE: you will need a printed pear macaron template that is easily accessible on the internet.

MACARON SHELLS:

Use my New Macaron Recipe at the beginning of this chapter on page 110

MINT WHITE CHOCOLATE GANACHE:

25 g fresh mint leaves

130 g heavy cream

110 g high quality white chocolate, chopped

PEAR FILLING:

2 pears washed, dried, hulled, and finely chopped into cubes

1 tsp. of honey or brown sugar

Pinch of cinnamon

Macaron Shells Directions:

1. Use my New Macaron Recipe from page 110 at the beginning of this chapter. Add 3-6 drops of neon green food coloring gel (or more, if desired) to the egg whites while also adding the sugar/egg white powder mixture. Once the macaronage has been completed, prepare the piping bag fitted with your 10 or 11 piping tips.
2. Fill the piping bag with the macaron batter and pipe the pear macaron shells using a printed template placed under your silicone mat. Not required/optional: rest/dry the piped macaron shells for 30-40 minutes before baking.

Mint White Chocolate Ganache Directions:

1. Add the heavy cream and the mint leaves to a medium pot. Place it on low heat and bring to a boil. Remove from the stove and set aside for 5 minutes.
2. Place the pot back onto the low heat and bring to a boil one more time. Take it off the heat and pour the heavy cream through the mesh sifter over the chopped white chocolate, catching the mint leaves in the sifter. Set it aside for 5 minutes to rest, and then mix well with a silicone spatula until all the white chocolate has melted and combined with the mint heavy cream.
3. Cover it with kitchen plastic/cling film making sure that the plastic is fully covering and laying over the surface of the ganache. Place into the refrigerator for 10–12 hours to set.
4. Once 10–12 hours have passed, whip the cold ganache with a hand or stand mixer for about 1 minute. Make sure not to overmix.

Pear Filling Directions:

1. Combine the cubed pears, honey/sugar, and cinnamon in a medium sized pot. Bring to a boil on low heat, occasionally stirring.
2. Once the mixture starts bubbling, remove from the heat and transfer it to a heatproof container. Allow it to cool to room temperature before using.

Assembly:

1. To make the stems: pipe or spread melted dark or milk chocolate on parchment paper. Place them into the refrigerator to set before use.
2. Fit the piping bag with #10 or #11 piping tips by Wilton and the whipped mint ganache. Pipe a ring of mint ganache along the edges of each half of the pre-matched pear macaron shells. Place some pear filling in the center. Cover it with the matching half of the macaron shell, pressing lightly. Add the chocolate stem.
3. Refrigerate the filled macarons for at least 24 hours so the shells get to absorb the filling and develop the flavors. Macarons taste their best after 24 hours of refrigeration, followed by warming up to room temperature for at least 30 minutes before consumption.

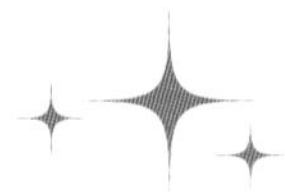

COCONUT RASPBERRY MACARONS

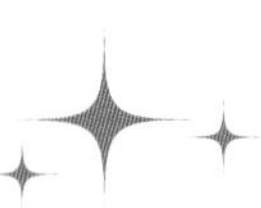

WHITE MACARON SHELLS:

Use my New Macaron Recipe at the beginning of this chapter on page 110

COCONUT BUTTERCREAM:

226 g (2 sticks) unsalted butter, at room temperature

397 g (1 can) sweetened condensed milk, at room temperature

1 tsp. coconut extract/flavoring

50 g of unsweetened shredded coconut, powdered in a food processor or blender

RASPBERRY CREAM:

180 g fresh or frozen raspberries, chopped

80 g sugar

2 egg yolks

30 g cornstarch

85 g unsalted butter, at room temperature

Pro Tip:

1. If your oven is hot/strong and your white macarons typically "brown" during baking, place a domed aluminum foil over the white macarons after 10–15 minutes of baking. You may also try baking the white macarons with the following setting: preheat the oven to 350 degrees Fahrenheit, place piped white macaron shells into the oven and immediately reduce the heat to 300 degrees Fahrenheit. Then bake for 25–27 minutes, also covering with the foil halfway through baking.

Coconut Buttercream Directions:

1. In the bowl of a mixer fitted with a whisk attachment, whip the butter for approximately 8 minutes until it has tripled in volume and become light and fluffy. Stop to scrape the bottom of the bowl a few times.
2. Reduce the speed of the mixer to low and add the sweetened condensed milk in thirds, whipping for about 8–10 seconds after each addition. Don't forget to scrape the bottom of the bowl after each addition.
3. While the mixer is running on low speed, add the coconut flavoring or extract and the powdered coconut. Allow to whip on low speed for additional 1–2 minutes.

Raspberry Cream Directions:

1. Add the raspberries and half of the sugar to a medium sized pan, bring to a boil. Keep boiling on medium heat for about 6–8 minutes.
2. Remove the reduced raspberries from the heat and puree them with an emerging blender or in a food processor. Set them aside.
3. Whip the egg yolks, corn starch, and the other half of the sugar to a uniform light consistency.
4. While continuously whisking the egg yolk mixture, slowly drizzle the raspberry puree into it
5. Return this mixture to the medium pot and heat it on medium heat, while continuously whisking, until it thickens.
6. Remove the mixture from the heat; transfer it to a heatproof container. Cover it with kitchen plastic/cling film—making sure that the plastic is touching the full surface of the cream. Set it aside until it cools off to room temperature.
7. Add the cubed butter and whip it with a hand or stand mixer for about one minute.

Assembly:

1. Fit two piping bags with small round tips, such as 10 or 11 by Wilton. Add the coconut buttercream to one and the raspberry cream into the other. Pipe a ring of the coconut buttercream along the outside edge of the halves of the pre-matched macaron shells. Pipe a dollop of raspberry cream in the center. Cover it with the matching half of the macaron shell, pressing lightly.
2. Refrigerate the filled macarons for at least 24 hours so the shells get to absorb the filling and develop the flavors. Macarons taste their best after 24 hours of refrigeration, followed by warming up to room temperature for at least 30 minutes before consumption.

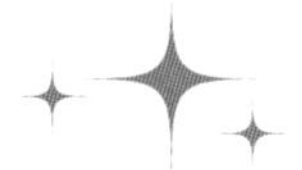

BLACKBERRY MACARONS

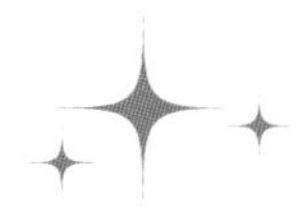

NOTE: this macaron recipe uses my original technique that does not include the use of black food coloring gel. Instead, it combines the Dutch processed black cocoa and food grade charcoal. Alternatively, you may use my new macaron recipe from page 110 at the beginning of this chapter. Add 8 grams of unsweetened cocoa to the dry ingredients and 10–20 drops of Super Black or Charcoal Black food coloring gel by Chefmaster.

BLACKBERRY MACARON SHELLS:

100 g fresh egg whites, at room temperature (divided: 50 g for Italian meringue, 50 g for almond paste)

40 g filtered or bottled water

130 g sugar

130 g powdered sugar

130 g almond flour (not almond meal)

8 g food grade charcoal

16 g Dutch processed black cocoa powder

BLACKBERRY WHIPPED GANACHE:

60 g pureed blackberries

55 g heavy cream

10 g butter

10 g light glucose syrup

125 g high quality white chocolate, chopped

GARNISH:

Fresh blackberries

Black Macaron Shells Directions:

1. Prepare the sugar syrup: Add sugar and water into your small pot, do not stir. Bring them to a boil on medium heat until it reaches 244 degrees Fahrenheit on your laser or candy thermometer. I prefer to use a laser thermometer from Home Depot or Amazon.

2. While your sugar syrup is getting to the boiling stage, prepare the Italian meringue. Add the first half of the egg whites into a grease-free, clean, dry stand mixer bowl. Start mixing it at low speed until egg whites start forming bubbles. Gradually increase the speed to medium. Once your egg whites start foaming—increase the speed to high and mix them until they become extremely foamy and frothy. Once your sugar syrup reaches 244 degrees Fahrenheit, slowly pour it in a steady, slow, thin stream right on the egg whites area between the whisk and the bowl while the mixer is continuously whisking it on high. Be careful not to pour your sugar syrup on the whisk. Once all the syrup is added, decrease the mixing speed to medium and mix it for approximately 6–8 minutes, until stiff peaks are achieved. Stop mixing when stiff peaks stage is achieved—overmixing will result in cracked or hollow macaron shells.

3. Preheat your oven to non-convectional (no fan) baking to 350 degrees Fahrenheit with one flat oven tray or cookie baking sheet on the center rack, heating it up with the oven. You will be baking your macarons on doubled up trays to prevent lopsided macaron shells. Note: this is a temperature and baking time that works for my oven. Below I will be discussing variations of oven temperatures and baking times.

4. While your Italian meringue is getting to stiff peaks, prepare almond paste. Sift together your charcoal powder, cocoa, powdered sugar, and almond flour, discarding any large pieces that do not freely pass through the mesh sifter (shouldn't be more than 1 tablespoon). Add your half of the room temperature egg whites and mix it with a silicon spatula until they are all combined and resemble a paste. At this point you can add a few drops of your preferred food coloring gel or powder, if desired. Cover it with a kitchen towel or cling film while your Italian meringue is whisking, getting to stiff peaks. Once your Italian meringue is ready, add it to the almond paste in three steps. First the two parts of the meringue can be mixed thoroughly, to loosen up the almond paste—you do not have to be careful here. Once you add the third, remaining part of meringue, your macaronage starts then. Your goal is to remove the air bubbles without overmixing, by pressing and turning the macaron batter to the side of your bowl. Every 3 turns check it for readiness. Your batter is fully ready when it freely flows from your spatula as a thin ribbon, and fully flattens in 10 seconds. Another test is to try drawing the number 8 with the batter flowing from your spatula onto the bowl.
5. Add your macaron batter to a piping bag fitted with a 0.5 cm round piping tip. Pipe the macarons onto a silicone macaron mat placed onto your second oven tray/sheet. I do not recommend using parchment paper. Holding your piping bag perpendicular to the baking mat, slowly pipe the macaron shells, releasing with a wiping motion. Tap your baking sheet/tray with the piped macaron shells on the counter a few times to remove any air bubbles. You can also use a toothpick to pop any remaining air bubbles. Rest your piped macaron shells for 30 to 60 minutes until the batter forms a skin/doesn't stick and loses some of its shine. Note: if you do not have a templated silicone macaron mat, below are printable templates for classic round and heart macarons. I bake my macarons at 350 degrees Fahrenheit for 10–12 minutes (depending on the thickness of your oven tray/baking sheet), turning halfway (more regarding this below). Allow the baked macarons to fully cool off before taking them off your macaron mats and filling.

IMPORTANT BAKING TEMPERATURES AND TIMES VARIATIONS:

350 degrees Fahrenheit for 10–12 minutes – best for large, spacious ovens (my preferred temp/time)

325 degrees Fahrenheit for 12–14 minutes – great as a standard starting point

300 degrees Fahrenheit for 16–18 minutes – best for white, light-colored macarons

275 degrees Fahrenheit for 18–20 minutes – most suitable for smaller ovens

Blackberry Whipped Ganace Directions:

1. Place the pureed blackberries into a small pot and bring them to a boil over low heat.
2. Combine the heavy cream and glucose, bring to a boil, and immediately pour over the white chocolate. Add the hot blackberry puree.
3. Mix well to combine with a silicone spatula. Add the cubed butter and mix again to combine.
4. Cover it with kitchen plastic/cling film over the surface of the ganache and refrigerate it for at least 4 hours.
5. After, whip the cold set ganache to a fluffy strong cream using a hand or stand mixer. Whip only for 1 minute or so, making sure not to overmix.

Assembly:

1. Fit the piping bag with the 8B piping tip by Wilton and the whipped blackberry ganache. Pipe "Hershey kisses" like dollops in the center of each half of the pre-matched macaron shells. Cover it with the matching half of the macaron shell, pressing lightly.
2. Refrigerate the filled macarons for at least 24 hours so the shells get to absorb the filling and develop the flavors. Macarons taste their best after 24 hours of refrigeration, followed by warming up to room temperature for at least 30 minutes before consumption.
3. Garnish the top of assembled macarons with the piped blackberry ganache and fresh blackberries.

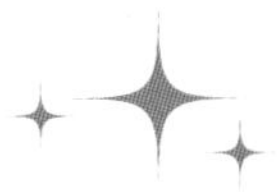

CARIBBEAN DELIGHT MACARONS

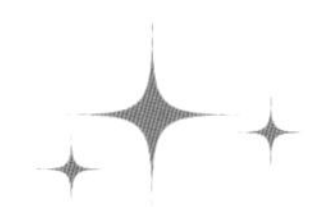

MACARON SHELLS:

Use my New Macaron Recipe at the beginning of this chapter on page 110

MANGO-PASSIONFRUIT WHIPPED GANACHE:

30 g mango puree (you may use fresh or frozen mango slices for the puree)

30 g passionfruit puree (you may use a ready-to-use passionfruit puree by Goya or make it yourself by pulverizing/pureeing fresh seedless passionfruit)

55 g heavy cream

10 g butter

10 g light glucose syrup

125 g high quality white chocolate, chopped

GARNISH:

Sparkling sugars or sugar pearls

Macaron Shells Directions:

1. Use my New Macaron Recipe from page 110. Once the macronage has been completed, prepare the piping bag fitted with your 10 or 11 piping tip. Using a food safe brush and the inside of the piping bag, draw two opposite lines with blue food coloring gel, two opposite lines of pink food coloring gel in between the blue ones, and two opposite lines of orange food coloring gel in between the pink and blue.
2. Fill the piping bag with the macaron batter and pipe the macaron shells as advised in the main/base recipe. Not required/optional: rest/dry the piped macaron shells for 30–40 minutes before baking.

Mango-Passionfruit Whipped Ganache Directions:

1. Place the pureed mango and passionfruit into a small pot and bring to a boil over low heat.
2. Combine the heavy cream and glucose, bring to a boil, and immediately pour over the white chocolate. Add the heated mango/passionfruit puree.
3. Mix well to combine with a silicone spatula. Add the cubed butter and mix again to combine.
4. Cover it with kitchen plastic/cling film over the surface of the ganache and refrigerate for at least 4 hours.
5. After, whip the cold set ganache to a fluffy strong cream using a hand or stand mixer. Whip only for 1 minute or so, making sure not to overmix.

Assembly:

1. Fit the piping bag with the 1M piping tip by Wilton and the whipped mango-passionfruit ganache. Pipe tall rosettes in the center of each half of the pre-matched macaron shells. Optional: sprinkle the piped ganache with sparkling sugars or sugar pearl. Cover it with the matching half of the macaron shell, pressing lightly.
2. Refrigerate the filled macarons for at least 24 hours so the shells get to absorb the filling and develop the flavors. Macarons taste their best after 24 hours of refrigeration, followed by warming up to room temperature for at least 30 minutes before consumption.

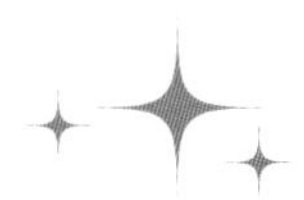

EARL GREY BLACK CURRANT MACARONS

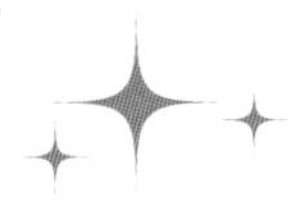

MACARON SHELLS:

Use my New Macaron Recipe at the beginning of this chapter on page 110

3 grams of powdered Earl Grey tea (or black tea, if desired)

BLACK CURRANT GANACHE:

60 g black currant puree

55 g heavy cream

10 g butter

10 g light glucose syrup

125 g high quality white chocolate, chopped

GARNISH:

Powdered Earl Grey tea

Macaron Shells Directions:

1. Use my New Macaron Recipe from page 110. Add 3 grams of powdered Earl Grey tea (or black tea, if desired) to the dry ingredients during the second sifting. Add 3 drops of black food coloring gel to the macaron batter during the macaronage to achieve the light grey color of the macarons.
2. Once the macaronage has been completed, prepare the piping bag fitted with your 10 or 11 piping tips. Fill the piping bag with the macaron batter and pipe the macaron shells as advised in the main/base recipe. Not required/optional: rest/dry the piped macaron shells for 30–40 minutes before baking.

Black Currant Ganache Directions:

1. Place the pureed black currants into a small pot and bring to a boil over low heat.
2. Combine the heavy cream and glucose, bring to a boil, and immediately pour over the white chocolate. Add the heated black currant puree.
3. Mix well to combine with a silicone spatula. Add the cubed butter and mix again to combine.
4. Cover it with kitchen plastic/cling film over the surface of the ganache and refrigerate for at least 4 hours.
5. After, whip the cold set ganache to a fluffy strong cream using a hand or stand mixer. Whip only for 1 minute or so, making sure not to overmix.

Assembly:

1. Fit a piping bag with a large round piping tip, such as 1A or 2A by Wilton, and add the black currant ganache. Pipe "Hershey kisses" like dollops in the center of each half of the pre-matched macaron shells. Cover it with the matching half of the macaron shell, pressing lightly.
2. Dust the filled/assembled macarons with powdered Earl Grey tea.
3. Refrigerate the filled macarons for at least 24 hours so the shells get to absorb the filling and develop the flavors. Macarons taste their best after 24 hours of refrigeration, followed by warming up to room temperature for at least 30 minutes before consumption.

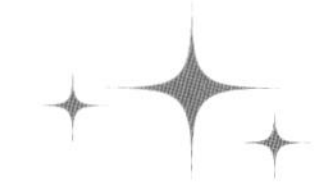

RASPBERRY CHOCOLATE CRUNCH MACARONS

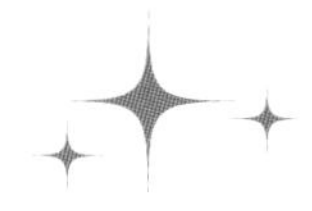

RASPBERRY MACARON SHELLS:

Use my New Macaron Recipe at the beginning of this chapter on page 110

3 grams of powdered freeze-dried raspberries

EGGLESS CHOCOLATE BUTTERCREAM:

1 can (397 g) sweetened condensed milk, at room temperature

375 g unsalted butter, at room temperature

3–5 Tbsp. unsweetened cocoa powder

GARNISH:

Powdered freeze-dried raspberries

Macaron Shells Directions:

1. Use my New Macaron Recipe from page 110. Add 3 grams of powdered freeze-dried raspberries to the dry ingredients during the second sifting. Add 6–8 drops of burgundy food coloring gel to the macaron batter during the macaronage.
2. Once the macaronage has been completed, prepare the piping bag fitted with your 10 or 11 piping tips. Fill the piping bag with the macaron batter and pipe the macaron shells as advised in the main/base recipe. Not required/optional: rest/dry the piped macaron shells for 30–40 minutes before baking.

Eggless Chocolate Buttercream Directions:

1. Add all the ingredients to the mixer bowl, fitted with a whisk attachment, and mix on high speed for approximately 5 minutes until it doubles in volume and becomes fluffy and silky.

Assembly:

1. Fit the piping bag with the 1M piping tip by Wilton and the whipped chocolate buttercream frosting. Pipe tall rosettes in the center of each half of the pre-matched raspberry macaron shells. Optional: sprinkle the piped chocolate frosting with crunchy chocolate pearls (Callebaut Chocolate or Valrhona). Cover it with the matching half of the macaron shell, pressing lightly.
2. Dust the filled/assembled macarons with powdered freeze-dried raspberries.
3. Refrigerate the filled macarons for at least 24 hours so the shells get to absorb the filling and develop the flavors. Macarons taste their best after 24 hours of refrigeration, followed by warming up to room temperature for at least 30 minutes before consumption.

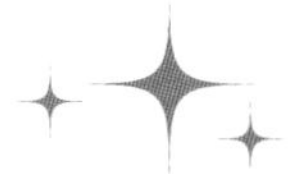

REUSE REDUCE MACARON SHELLS

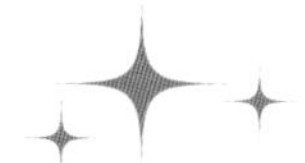

NOTE: you can halve this recipe, yielding 25 macarons (50 macaron shells)

This is my tried-and-true Macaron Recipe that includes re-using your previously (badly) baked macaron shells. Yes, you heard that right. Perfecting your macaron shells, aiming for achievement of those desirable cute ruffly feet, smooth tops, and avoiding hollows is a tricky process. It includes not only properly weighed ingredients and mastering macronage, but also tirelessly playing with your oven temperatures. The success of the macarons depends not only on the humidity in your work area, but also how strong and spacious your oven is. And I want you to continue practicing until you find your perfect oven temperature and not get discouraged if all your macaron shells do not turn out "Instagram worthy." You can reuse them for making a new macaron batch. Unbelievable, right? You'll believe me once you try this recipe.

It has been over two years since I started making macarons almost every day. I've mastered French, Italian, and Swiss methods, used dozens of different mats, oven trays, hundreds of food gels, and brands of ingredients. If my macaron shells did not turn out perfectly and no one could eat them anymore, I unfortunately had to discard them (just as many of you did, I'm sure). This left me concerned for many reasons and prompted looking for all possible ways to salvage this situation, giving assurance that I can continue practicing and perfecting my macarons and not waste ingredients or time doing so. This is a solution and assurance for all of you as well. If you need to continue practicing and learning how to make macarons, or even if you are a seasoned macaron baker that sometimes faces these "moody, finicky, temperamental little cookies" fails—do not overheat or ever throw them away. Instead, save them and use to make a new batch with the following recipe.

MACARON SHELLS:

200 g fresh egg whites, at room temperature (divided: 100 g for Italian meringue, 100 g for almond paste)

80 g filtered or bottled water

260 g sugar

150 g finely crushed dry baked macaron shells (weigh after crushing)

185 g powdered sugar

185 g almond flour (not almond meal)

Optional: gel or powder food coloring (I prefer Americolor Food Gels or The Sugar Art Elite Colors.)—only if you are reusing white badly baked macaron shells. If you are re-using your colored shells you can enhance the same color by adding food gel or powder in this process or change it, if desired. For example, if I am reusing pink macarons shells here, I may add blue food gel or powder to result in purple macarons.

Macaron Shells Directions:

1. Prepare the sugar syrup: Add sugar and water into your small pot, do not stir. Bring to a boil on medium heat until it reaches 244 degrees Fahrenheit on your laser or candy thermometer. I prefer to use a laser thermometer from Home Depot or Amazon.
2. While your sugar syrup is getting to the boiling stage, prepare the Italian meringue. Add 100 grams of fresh room temperature egg whites into a grease-free, clean, dry stand mixer bowl. Start mixing at low speed until the egg whites start forming bubbles. Gradually increase the speed to medium. Once your egg whites start foaming up—increase the speed to high and mix until they become foamy and frothy. Once your sugar syrup reaches 244 degrees Fahrenheit, slowly pour it in a steady, slow, thin stream right on the egg white area between the whisk and the bowl while the mixer is continuously whisking on high. Be careful not to pour your sugar syrup on the whisk. Once all the syrup is added, decrease the mixing speed to medium and mix for approximately 6–8 minutes, until stiff peaks

are achieved. Stop mixing when the stiff peak stage is achieved—overmixing will result in cracked or hollow macaron shells.

3. Preheat your oven to non-convectional (no fan) baking at 350 degrees Fahrenheit with one flat oven tray or cookie baking sheet on the center rack, heating it up with the oven. You will be baking your macarons on doubled up trays to prevent lopsided macaron shells. Note: this is a temperature and baking time that works for my oven. Below I will be discussing variations of oven temperatures and baking times.
4. While your Italian meringue is getting to stiff peaks, prepare the almond paste.
5. Crush your "badly baked" macaron shells (no feet, cracked tops, hollow insides) in a food processor to a fine, powder-like consistency. I prefer to use a "Magic Bullet" or "Ninja" smoothie blending cup. Note: your macaron shells must be fully baked/cooled/dry. If your macarons have not baked inside or are sticky—bake them again for a few more minutes or leave out overnight. The macaron shells must be dry and hard. Measure 150 grams. Usually that is 1 macaron made of shells, approximately 20–24 macarons.
6. Sift together your 150 grams of ground macaron shells, 185 grams of powdered sugar and 185 grams of almond flour, discarding any large pieces that do not freely pass through the mesh sifter. Add your other 100 grams of room temperature egg whites and mix with a silicon spatula until it is all combined and resembles a paste. At this point you can add a few drops of your preferred food coloring gel or powder, if desired. Cover it with a kitchen towel or cling film while your Italian meringue is whisking, getting to stiff peaks. Once your Italian meringue is ready, add it to the almond paste in three steps. First two parts of the meringue can be mixed thoroughly, to loosen up the almond paste—you do not have to be careful here. Once you add the third, remaining part of meringue, your macaronage starts. Your goal is to remove any air bubbles without overmixing, by pressing and turning the macaron batter to the side of your bowl. Every 3 turns check it for readiness. Your batter is fully ready when it freely flows from your spatula as a thin ribbon, and fully flattens in 10 seconds. Another test is to try drawing the number 8 with the batter flowing from your spatula onto the bowl.
7. Add your macaron batter to a piping bag fitted with 0.5 cm round piping tip. Pipe the macarons onto a silicone macaron mat placed onto your second oven tray/sheet. I do not recommend using parchment paper. Holding your piping bag perpendicular to the baking mat, slowly pipe circles, releasing them with a wiping motion. Tap your baking sheet/tray with the piped macaron shells on the counter a few times to remove air bubbles. You can also use a toothpick to pop any remaining air bubbles. Rest your piped macaron shells for 30 to 60 minutes until the batter forms a skin/doesn't stick and loses some of its shine. Note: If you do not have a templated silicone macaron mat, below are printable templates for classic round and heart macarons. I bake my macarons at 350 degrees Fahrenheit for 10–12 minutes (depending on the thickness of your oven tray/baking sheet), turning halfway (more regarding this below). Allow the baked macarons to fully cool off before taking them off your macaron mats and filling.
8. Fill with your favorite buttercreams, ganache, creams, caramels, reductions, or curds. The flavor possibilities are endless.

IMPORTANT BAKING TEMPERATURE AND TIME VARIATIONS

350 degrees Fahrenheit for 10–12 minutes – best for large, spacious ovens (my preferred temp/time)

325 degrees Fahrenheit for 12–14 minutes – great as a standard starting point

300 degrees Fahrenheit for 16–18 minutes – best for white or light-colored macarons

275 degrees Fahrenheit for 18–20 minutes – most suitable for smaller ovens

CHAPTER 6

The Magic of Pastries

MINI TARTS, SIGNATURE HEART CAKE, AND PATE CHOUX (12 RECIPES), INCLUDING SUGAR-FREE INSTRUCTIONS

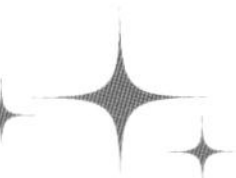

PASSIONFRUIT FIG MINI TART

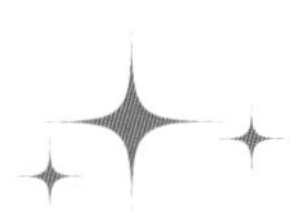

Weighing in grams is essential for the precision and successful result of this recipe. Measurements in cups are not included, nor recommended. *PRO TIP: For Gluten Free version of this recipe, simply substitute the all-purpose flour with 1:1 Gluten Free flour.

SWEET PASTRY TART SHELLS:

125 g all-purpose flour

30 g almond flour

50 g powdered sugar

75 g butter, cold and cubed

1 pinch of salt

½ egg, beaten

PASSIONFRUIT GANACHE:

60 g fresh or frozen seedless passionfruit puree

55 g heavy cream

10 g butter

125 g high quality white chocolate, chopped

Sweet Pastry Tart Shells Directions:

1. Preheat the oven to 350 degrees Fahrenheit.
2. In the food processor or blender, pulse the flour, almond flour, powdered sugar, salt and butter for a few seconds until combined.
3. Add the egg and continue processing until the dough forms a ball.
4. Remove the dough from the food processor/ blender and wrap it into kitchen plastic/ cling film. Place it into the refrigerator for 30 minutes to set.
5. Once the dough has chilled in the refrigerator, cut it into small pieces to soften a bit, then form a ball again and roll it between two pieces of parchment paper to approximately ¼ inch thickness. Place it into the refrigerator for 30–60 minutes to firm it up.
6. Fill your mini tart pans/molds or rings placed over the silicone or mesh baking mats, with the dough. Carefully and gently even out the dough on the bottom and sides of the pans/ molds or tart rings.
7. Use a fork to lightly prick the bottoms.
8. Place the filled pans/rings into the freezer for 15 minutes so they firm up before you start perfecting the edges. Using a sharp knife and holding it perfectly perpendicular to the tart ring, slice out the excess dough that came out from the sides of the pans/rings.
9. Bake the tarts on the middle rack of the oven for approximately 10–15 minutes until they turn to a light golden color. Let them cool completely before removing them from the pans/rings.

Passionfruit GanacheDirections:

1. Bring the passionfruit puree to a boil.
2. Separately heat the heavy cream in the microwave or on the stove.
3. Pour both liquids over the white chocolate. Mix well with a silicone spatula until all the ingredients have combined to a uniform, smooth finish.
4. Add the cubed butter. Mix well with your silicone spatula until combined.

Assembly:

1. Fill cooled tart shells with the warm passionfruit ganache. Place the filled tarts into the refrigerator for at least one hour to allow the ganache to set and harden.
2. Decorate with a slice of fresh or freeze dried figs.

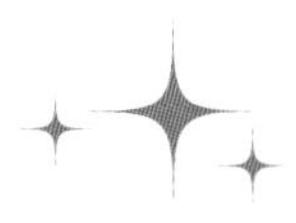

HAZELNUT STRAWBERRY CHOCOLATE MINI TART

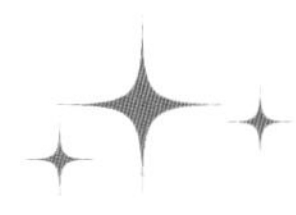

Weighing in grams is essential for the precision and successful result of this recipe. Measurements in cups are not included, nor recommended. *PRO TIP: For Gluten Free version of this recipe, simply substitute the all-purpose flour with 1:1 Gluten Free flour.

CHOCOLATE PATE SUCRE (SWEET PASTRY):

110 g all-purpose flour

50 g powdered sugar

20 g cocoa powder

25 g almond flour

75 g unsalted butter, cold and cubed

½ egg, at room temperature, beaten

HAZELNUT PRALINE:

100 g raw or lightly roasted unsalted hazelnuts

90 g granulated sugar

STRAWBERRY CREAM:

180 g strawberries, fresh or frozen, chopped

80 g granulated sugar

2 egg yolks

30 g cornstarch

85 g unsalted butter, at room temperature

GARNISH:

Baked meringue kisses

Whole hazelnuts

Chocolate Pate Sucre Tart Shells Directions:

1. Preheat the oven to 350 degrees Fahrenheit.
2. In the food processor or blender, pulse the flour, almond flour, powdered sugar, cocoa powder and butter for a few seconds until combined.
3. Add the egg and continue processing until the dough forms a ball.
4. Remove the dough from the food processor/blender and wrap it into kitchen plastic/cling film. Place into the refrigerator for 30 minutes to set.
5. Once the dough has chilled in the refrigerator, cut it into small pieces to soften a bit, then form a ball again and roll it between two pieces of parchment paper to approximately ¼ inch thickness. Place it into the refrigerator for 30-60 minutes to firm it up.
6. Drape your mini tart pans/molds or rings placed over the silicone or mesh baking mats, with the dough. Carefully and gently even out the dough on the bottom and sides of the pans/molds or tart rings. Make sure not to stretch the dough too much, otherwise, it will shrink during the baking.
7. Use a fork to lightly prick the bottoms.
8. Place the filled pans/rings into the freezer for 15 minutes so they firm up before you start perfecting the edges. Using a sharp knife and holding it perfectly perpendicular to the tart ring, slice out the excess dough that came out from the sides of the pans/rings.
9. Bake the tarts on the middle rack of the oven for approximately 10-15 minutes until crispy.
10. Let them cool completely before removing them from the pans/rings.

Hazelnut Praline Directions:

1. Combine hazelnuts and sugar in a saucepan and place it over medium heat.
2. Once the sugar begins to caramelize, stir to coat all the hazelnuts evenly.
3. Transfer onto a silicone baking mat or parchment paper and let it cool.
4. Once the brittle has fully cooled off—break it into pieces.
5. Transfer it into a blender and blend on medium speed until it reaches a paste consistency.

Strawberry Cream Directions:

1. Add the strawberries and half of the sugar to the medium sized pan, bring to a boil. Keep boiling on medium heat for about 6-8 minutes.
2. Remove the reduced strawberries from the heat and puree with an emerging blender or in a food processor. Set aside.
3. Whip the egg yolks, corn starch, and the other half of the sugar to a uniform light consistency.
4. While continuously whisking the egg yolk mixture, slowly drizzle the strawberry puree into it. Return this mixture to the medium pot and heat it on medium heat, while continuously whisking, until it thickens.
5. Remove the mixture from the heat; transfer it to a heatproof container. Cover it with kitchen plastic/cling film—making sure that the plastic is touching the full surface of the cream. Set it aside until it cools off to room temperature. Add the cubed butter and whip with a hand or stand mixer for about one minute.

Assembly:

1. Press the hazelnut praline onto the bottoms of the cooled chocolate tart shells. Using a piping bag fitted with an 8B piping tip and strawberry cream, pipe the dollops of strawberry cream over the praline to fill the tart. Decorate with baked meringue kisses and whole hazelnuts.

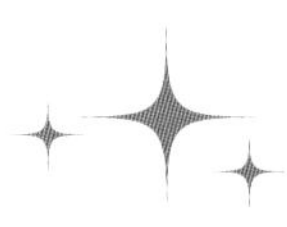

SIGNATURE HEART TART CAKE WITH "ICE-CREAM" CREAM

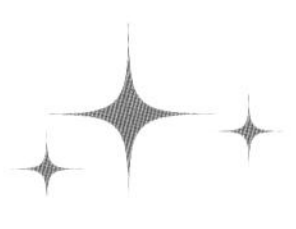

Weighing in grams is essential for the precision and successful result of this recipe. Measurements in cups are not included, nor recommended. *PRO TIP: For Gluten Free version of this recipe, simply substitute the all-purpose flour with 1:1 Gluten Free flour.

TART DOUGH:

280 g all-purpose flour

200 g unsalted butter, cold

50 g powdered sugar

2 Tbsp. granulated sugar

Pinch of salt

1 egg (beaten)

1 tsp. pure vanilla extract

"ICE CREAM" CREAM:

500 r mascarpone cheese, cold

1 Tbsp. of sour cream or Greek yogurt, cold

250 g heavy cream, cold

240 g powdered sugar

1 tsp. of pure vanilla extract (clear preferred)

GARNISH:

Fresh fruit and berries

Candies

Macarons

Heart Tart Directions:

1. Add the flour, powdered sugar, granulated sugar, and salt to your mixer bowl and stir on low speed with pedal attachment for 1 minute.
2. While still stirring on low speed, add the cubed cold butter 1 tablespoon at a time. Continue stirring it for about 5 minutes until the mixture resembles a cornmeal like texture.
3. Add 1 beaten egg and vanilla, while still stirring on low speed. The dough will come together quickly at this point, do not overmix.
4. As soon as the dough starts coming off the sides of the bowl, turn off the mixer and transfer all the dough onto the plastic wrap. Loosely form a ball, wrap it into the plastic wrap and refrigerate for 30–60 minutes.
5. After the dough has firmed up in the refrigerator, remove it from the plastic wrap and cut it into 2 equal halves. Roll each half between 2 sheets of parchment paper to make an approximately ¼ inch thick rectangle. Refrigerate both rolled dough sheets for 30 minutes.
6. Preheat your oven to 350 degrees Fahrenheit.
7. Remove the refrigerated rolled dough from the refrigerator. Using a small pear knife, cut each of the sheets into a large heart free-hand or using a printed template. Bake for 20 minutes. Turn the baking sheet around halfway through cooking time. Let it cool completely on the cooling rack.

"Ice Cream" Cream Directions:

1. Add all ingredients into your mixer bowl and mix with a whisk attachment on low speed. Slowly increase to high speed for about 5 minutes or until the cream has thickened and doubled in volume. Make sure not to overmix.
2. As soon as the cream doubles in volume, becomes light, fluffy, and airy, with the whisk attachment leaving ruffle indentations while mixing—stop the mixer.

Assembly:

1. Fit a piping bag with a 1A or 2A piping tip by Wilton and the cream. Pipe the dollops of the cream on the back of one of the baked/cooled heart tarts.
2. Place the tart onto the serving platter or the rectangle cake board. Pipe "Hershey kisses" like dollops along the outside edges of the tart first, followed by piping in between the piped edges. Place the second heart tart on top and repeat with the piping.
3. The decorating possibilities of these cakes are endless. You can use anything from fresh fruit, berries, and citruses to edible florals and greens, candies, chocolates, macarons, meringues, marshmallows, popcorn, cookies, and even other small treats like my peach cookies from chapter 2, or mini pavlovas.

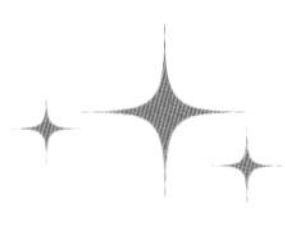

SUGAR-FREE CHOCOLATE HONEY CHRISTMAS TREE CAKE (MEDOVIK)

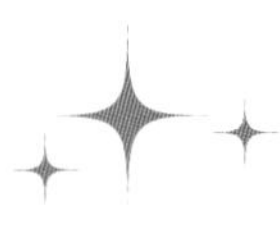

Weighing in grams is essential for the precision and successful result of this recipe. Measurements in cups are not included, nor recommended. *PRO TIP: For Gluten Free version of this recipe, simply substitute the all-purpose flour with 1:1 Gluten Free flour.

CHOCOLATE HONEY CAKEE:

270 g all-purpose flour

Pinch of salt

350 g honey

3 large eggs, at room temperature

2 tsp. baking soda

15 g vinegar

3 Tbsp. unsweetened cocoa powder

HONEY CREAM:

5 g gelatin powder or agar powder

30 g cold water

120 g cream cheese, at room temperature

120 g honey

200 g heavy cream, cold

250 g sour cream, cold

GARNISH:

Peeled mandarins, fresh mint leaves, and sparkling cranberries

Your favorite cookies, waffles, candies, and chocolates

Sugar-Free Honey Cream Directions:

1. Sprinkle the gelatin over cold water, mix to combine well and allow it to bloom for 5 minutes.
2. In the bowl of a stand mixer fitted with a whisk attachment, whip the cream cheese and honey on high speed until all is well combined.
3. Melt the bloomed gelatin in the microwave for 10–15 seconds, add it to the cream cheese/honey mixture and whip it on low speed.
4. In a separate bowl, whip the cold heavy cream to soft peaks and then add it to the cream cheese/honey mixture and the cold sour cream by hand with a silicone spatula.
5. Refrigerate this for at least 60 minutes while you are preparing/baking the honey cakes.

Sugar-Free Chocolate Honey Cake Layers Directions:

1. Pre-heat the oven to 350 degrees Fahrenheit.
2. Sift together the flour, cocoa, and salt and set aside.
3. Add the eggs to the bowl of a stand mixer fitted with a whisk attachment. Whip them on high speed for approximately 5 minutes until they double in volume and become lighter in color.
4. Reduce the mixer speed to low, add honey, and gradually increase the speed of the mixer to medium-high. Whip on medium-high speed for 6–8 minutes.
5. Lower the mixer speed to low. Combine the soda and vinegar and add it to the honey mixture.
6. Switch to the paddle attachment, and gradually add the dry ingredients while the mixer is still mixing on low speed. Mix until it all combines to a smooth batter.
7. Fill two greased Wilton's Christmas Tree baking pans with the chocolate honey batter, approximately to a quarter of an inch in thickness. Alternatively, you may bake the thin honey cake layers in sheet pans, cutting out the Christmas trees by hand or by using a printable template once they cool off.
8. Bake at 350 degrees Fahrenheit for 6–8 minutes on the middle rack till the honey cakes turn to a rich amber color.
9. Allow the baked cakes to fully cool off before removing them from the baking pans or baking sheet.

Assembly:

1. Smooth a thin layer of the honey filling on a 10-inch cake round. Place the first chocolate honey cake layer over it and lightly press, allowing it to adhere. Pipe hershey-kisses like dollops of honey cream with Wilton's 1A piping tip.
2. Repeat with the remaining cake and filling. Place the filled cake into the refrigerator for 30 minutes.
3. Decorate with peeled mandarins, fresh mint leaves, sparkling cranberries, and your favorite cookies, waffles, candies, chocolates if desired.

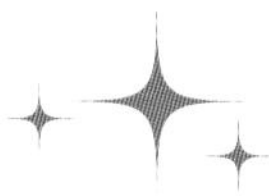

LAVENDER BLUEBERRY MINI PAVLOVA

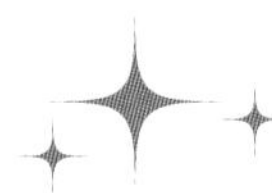

Weighing in grams is essential for the precision and successful result of this recipe. Measurements in cups are not included, nor recommended.

MERINGUE:

100 g fresh egg whites, at room temperature

200 g super fine/caster sugar

1 tsp. powdered lavender buds

Purple food coloring gel

VANILLA CHANTILLY CREAM:

250 g heavy cream, cold

50 g powdered sugar

1 tsp. of pure vanilla extract (clear preferred)

GARNISH:

Fresh blueberries

Lavender Mini Pavlova Directions:

1. Note: Separate your egg whites from the egg yolks while your eggs are cold. Leave the egg whites out to warm up to room temperature for at least an hour.
2. Preheat your oven on the convectional bake setting at 200 degrees Fahrenheit.
3. Prepare the double boiler. I use a pot slightly larger in diameter than my mixing bowl. Fill it with a bit of water and place it on medium-high heat.
4. Wipe your mixing bowl and whisk attachment with a bit of lemon juice on a piece of paper towel. Pour your room temperature egg whites and superfine sugar into your mixing bowl and place into a pot with boiling water. Make that sure your mixing bowl with the egg whites and sugar does not touch the boiling water. Reduce the heat to medium-low to ensure that the water is barely simmering.
5. Whisk your egg whites/sugar mixture with your whisk nonstop for 2.5–3 minutes. I use the whisk mixer attachment—fewer steps, fewer dishes to wash.
6. Transfer your mixing bowl onto the mixer and start mixing on a low speed for 30 seconds, gradually increasing the speed to medium. Add the powdered lavender buds and 6–8 drops of purple food coloring gel.
7. Gradually increase the speed to high. Mix on high speed for 8 minutes. You are looking for stiff meringue, meaning—when 8 minutes have passed, pull your whisk out and check the meringue's peak—it should just slightly curve.
8. Place the meringue into your piping bag fitted with a Wilton's 8B piping tip. I prefer to use my silicone baking mats for baking the meringue, but you can also use parchment paper. Here is a little tip to prevent your parchment paper from sliding on your baking tray when you pipe meringue—put a little drop or swipe of your meringue onto the baking tray under the parchment paper.
9. Pipe some large, tall meringue shells to about 3 inches in diameter. You should have two full circles of the piped meringue.
10. Bake for 60 minutes on the middle rack. Meringues are ready when you slightly push on them and they do not move or wiggle. If they are still wiggly—they need to be baked for a few more minutes.
11. Allow your meringues to fully cool off before removing them from your silicone mats or parchment paper. They can be eaten immediately or stored in an airtight container in a dark, dry, cool place for up to a month.

Vanilla Chantilly Cream Directions:

1. Add all ingredients into your mixer bowl and mix with a whisk attachment on low speed. Slowly increase to high speed for about 5 minutes until the cream has thickened and doubled in volume. Make sure not to overmix.
2. As soon as the cream doubles in volume, becomes light, fluffy, and airy, with the whisk attachment leaving ruffle indentations while mixing—stop the mixer.

Assembly:

1. To fill and decorate: using a 1M piping tip by Wilton, pipe tall rosettes/swirls of the Chantilly cream on top of the baked/cooled meringue shells, and top with fresh blueberries.

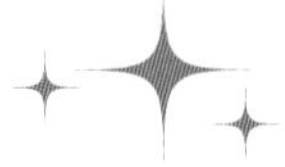

CHOCOLATE PISTACHIO MINI PAVLOVA

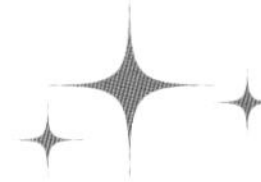

Weighing in grams is essential for the precision and successful result of this recipe. Measurements in cups are not included, nor recommended.

CHOCOLATE MINI PAVLOVA:

100 g fresh egg whites, at room temperature

200 g super fine/caster sugar

8 g unsweetened cocoa powder

CHOCOLATE PISTACHIO WHIPPED GANACHE:

220 g heavy cream, cold

100 g high quality milk chocolate

20 g pistachio paste

40 g unsalted butter, at room temperature

GARNISH:

Roasted or raw pistachios

Cocoa powder

Edible flowers (optional)

Chocolate Mini Pavlovas Directions:

1. Note: Separate your egg whites from the egg yolks while your eggs are cold. Leave the egg whites out to warm up to room temperature for at least an hour.
2. Preheat your oven on a convectional bake setting at 200 degrees Fahrenheit.
3. Prepare the double boiler. Use a pot slightly larger in diameter than mixing bowl. Fill it with a bit of water and place it on medium-high heat.
4. Wipe your mixing bowl and whisk attachment with a bit of lemon juice on piece of paper towel. Pour your room temperature egg whites and caster sugar into your mixing bowl and place into a pot with boiling water. Make sure that mixing bowl with egg whites and sugar does not touch the boiling water.

Reduce the heat to medium-low to ensure that the water is barely simmering.

5. Whisk your egg whites/sugar mixture with your whisk nonstop for 2.5–3 minutes. I use the whisk mixer attachment—fewer steps, fewer dishes to wash.

6. Transfer your mixing bowl onto the mixer and start mixing on low speed for 30 seconds, gradually increasing the speed to medium. Stop the mixer and add the cocoa powder, then start the mixer on low speed again and slowly increase to high. Mix on high speed for 8 minutes. You are looking for stiff meringue here, meaning—when 8 minutes have passed, pull your whisk out and check the meringue's peak—it should just slightly curve.

7. If using a silicone mat: place a 3 inch or larger circle printed template under the silicone mat to ensure that all the mini-Pavlovas match in size. If using parchment paper make the templates for the mini-Pavlovas by circling around a cookie cutter, mug, cup, or glass with a pen or a pencil. Flip the parchment paper unless you are using an edible marker. Place a large dollop/mountain of the chocolate meringue onto the circled templates. Using a small offset spatula or spoon, even out the mini-Pavlovas to keep them nice and round and within the templated circles. Swipe the sides of the mini-Pavlovas from bottom to the top to form and resemble a crown.

8. Bake for 60–75 minutes on the middle rack. Meringues are ready when you slightly push on them and they do not move. If they are still wiggly, they need to be baked for a few more minutes.

9. Allow your meringue to fully cool off before removing them from your silicone mats or parchment paper. They can be eaten immediately or stored in an airtight container in a dark, dry, cool place for up to a month.

10. *Pro Tip: to prevent your parchment paper from sliding on your baking tray when you pipe meringue—put a little drop or swipe of your meringue onto the baking tray under the parchment paper.

Chocolate Pistachio Whipped Ganache Directions:

1. Heat the heavy cream to just about boiling point and pour over the milk chocolate. Mix well with the silicone spatula.

2. Add pistachio paste and whip on low speed with a hand mixer or an emerging blender. Allow it to cool to room temperature.

3. Add the butter and whip again. Cover it with a kitchen plastic/cling film fully touching the surface of ganache. Place it into the refrigerator for at least 8 hours.

4. Once the ganache sets in the refrigerator, whip it again with the hand mixer or an emerging blender, for about 1 minute. Make sure not to overmix.

Assembly:

1. Fit the piping bag with an 8B piping tip by Wilton, and the chocolate pistachio ganache. Pipe dollops of the ganache inside if they crack, which is totally normal, and on the top surface of the cooled chocolate mini-Pavlovas.

2. Sprinkle with roasted or raw pistachios, cocoa powder, and edible flowers if desired.

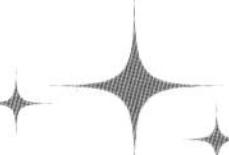

WHIPPED DOUBLE CHOCOLATE ECLAIRS

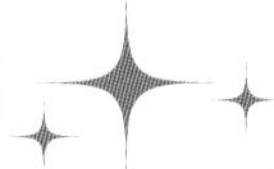

Weighing in grams is essential for the precision and successful result of this recipe. Measurements in cups are not included, nor recommended. *PRO TIP: For Gluten Free version of this recipe, simply substitute the all-purpose flour with 1:1 Gluten Free flour.

CHOUX PASTRY:

85 g water

85 g whole milk

85 g unsalted butter

2g salt

3g granulated sugar

85 g bread flour

140 g beaten whole eggs

SHINY CHOCOLATE GANACHE:

40 g heavy cream

10 g butter

10 g light glucose syrup

125 g high quality dark chocolate, chopped

Pinch of salt

WHIPPED WHITE GANACHE:

40 g heavy cream

10 g unsalted butter

10 g light glucose syrup

125 g high quality white chocolate, chopped

Pinch of salt

GARNISH:

Powdered sugar

Choux Pastry Directions:

1. Pre-heat the oven to non-convectional bake setting at 350 degrees Fahrenheit.
2. Sift the bread flour into a bowl, set it aside.
3. Add the water, milk, butter, sugar, and salt to a medium pan and place it on low heat, stirring occasionally. Bring it to a rolling boil. Immediately remove the pan from the heat, add the bread flour and stir well into the wet ingredients. Once no flour is showing and it is all absorbed, place the pan back on medium heat. Beat the mixture nonstop with a wooden spoon or silicone spatula until it slightly dries, about 2 minutes. Remove it from heat and transfer to the mixing bowl of stand mixer. Fit the mixer with pedal attachment and beat the dough on low speed for about 2–3 minutes (it should cool off to 115 degrees Fahrenheit).
4. Reduce the mixer speed to medium low and slowly pour the beaten eggs, a small amount at a time allowing each addition to incorporate with the rest of the ingredients.
5. Once all the eggs are added, the choux pastry dough should look creamy and not too runny.
6. Add the dough to a piping bag fitted with an 8B, 1A or 2A piping tip by Wilton. Pipe the eclairs onto the parchment paper, silicone, or perforated baking mat, leaving space between each one.
7. Dust the tops of the eclairs with powdered sugar. Open the oven and splash the bottom of the oven with about 2 tablespoons of water. Immediately place the baking sheet with piped eclairs onto the middle rack and close the oven—the steam promotes more even baking of the eclairs.
8. Bake for 60 minutes, do not open the oven at all during this time, otherwise, eclairs may not bake properly.
9. Once the eclairs have baked for 60 minutes to a deep golden color, remove them from the oven and allow them to fully cool off before removing them from the paper/mats.

Shiny Chocolate Ganache Directions:

1. Combine the heavy cream and the glucose, bring to a boil, and immediately pour over the chopped dark chocolate.
2. Mix well to combine with a silicone spatula. Add the cubed butter and mix again to combine.
3. Cover it with kitchen plastic/cling film over the surface of the ganache and set it aside.

Whipped White Ganache Directions:

1. Combine the heavy cream and the glucose, bring to a boil, and immediately pour over the white chocolate.
2. Mix well to combine with a silicone spatula. Add the cubed butter and mix again to combine.
3. Cover it with kitchen plastic/cling film over the surface of the ganache and refrigerate for at least 4 hours.
4. After, whip the cold set ganache to a fluffy strong cream using a hand or stand mixer. Whip only for 1 minute or so, making sure not to overmix.

Assembly:

1. Slice open (horizontally) the cooled eclairs with a sharp serrated knife. Using a piping bag fitted with #10 or #11 piping tip and the shiny chocolate ganache, pipe the bottom half of the sliced eclair.
2. Using a piping bag fitted with a 1M or 2D piping tip and the whipped white ganache, pipe ruffles, rosettes, or drop flowers over the dark chocolate ganache. Close with the other half of the cream puff. Place into the refrigerator for at least an hour to set.
3. Dust with powdered sugar before serving if desired.

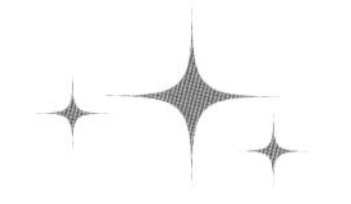

PEANUT BUTTER BLACK CURRANT CHOUX BUNS

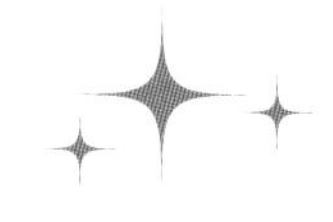

Where the version of the American classic meets a French pastry. These Choux Buns (cream puffs) are my ultimate ode to the PBJ sandwich, made with my favorite-black currant. If you have never tried this flavor combination you are missing out. Please give them a shot and thank me later.

Weighing in grams is essential for the precision and successful result of this recipe. Measurements in cups are not included, nor recommended. *PRO TIP: For Gluten Free version of this recipe, simply substitute the all-purpose flour with 1:1 Gluten Free flour.

CHOUX PASTRY:

85 g water

85 g whole milk

85 g unsalted butter

2g salt

3g granulated sugar

85 g bread flour

140 g beaten whole eggs

PEANUT BUTTER CHEESECAKE CREAM:

60 g smooth peanut butter

60 g cream cheese, softened

30 g powdered sugar

80 g heavy cream, cold

BLACK CURRANT CONFITURE:

250 g puree of fresh or frozen black currants

50 g granulated sugar

3 g lemon zest

8 g lemon juice

60 g water (divided in half)

15 g cornstarch

GARNISH:

Fresh or frozen black currants

Powdered sugar

Choux Pastry Directions:

1. Pre-heat the oven to non-convectional bake setting at 350 degrees Fahrenheit.
2. Sift the bread flour into a bowl, set it aside.
3. Add the water, milk, butter, sugar and salt to a medium pan and place it on low heat, stirring occasionally. Bring it to a rolling boil. Immediately remove the pan from the heat and add the bread flour and stir well into the wet ingredients. Once no flour is showing and it is all absorbed, place the pan back on medium heat. Beat the mixture nonstop with a wooden spoon or a silicone spatula until it slightly dries, about 2 minutes. Remove from the heat and transfer to the mixing bowl of stand mixer. Fit the mixer with pedal attachment and beat the dough on low speed for about 2–3 minutes (it should cool off to 115 degrees Fahrenheit).
4. Reduce the mixer speed to medium low and slowly pour the beaten eggs, a small amount at a time allowing each addition to incorporate to the rest of the ingredients.
5. Once all the eggs are added, the choux pastry dough should look creamy and not too runny.

6. Add the dough to a piping bag fitted with a 1A or 2A piping tip by Wilton. Pipe the cream puffs as round discs approximately 2 inches in diameter onto the parchment paper, silicone, or perforated baking mat, leaving space between them as they will expand during baking.
7. Dust the tops of the cream puffs with powdered sugar. Open the oven and splash the bottom of the oven with about 2 tablespoons of water. Immediately place the baking sheet with piped cream puffs onto the middle rack and close the oven—the steam in the oven promotes more even baking of the choux dough.
8. Bake for 60 minutes. Do not open the oven at all during this time, otherwise the cream puffs may not bake properly.
9. Once the puffs have baked for 60 minutes to a deep golden color, remove them from the oven and allow them to fully cool off before removing from the paper/mats.

Peanut Butter Cheesecake Cream Directions:

1. In the bowl of a stand mixer fitted with a whisk attachment, whip the peanut butter, cream cheese and powdered sugar until it is all smooth and combined.
2. In a separate bowl, whip the cold heavy cream to stiff peaks.
3. Fold in the whipped cream into the peanut butter mixture in 3 steps. Place into the refrigerator until ready to use.

Black Currant Confiture Directions:

1. Place the black currant puree, sugar, lemon zest, lemon juice, and 30 grams of water into a medium sized pot and bring to a boil on medium heat, constantly mixing with a silicone spatula.
2. Once boiling, reduce the heat to medium-low and allow to cook for 10–15 minutes.
3. Remove the pot from the stove and immediately strain the confiture into a separate heatproof bowl, making sure all the currants are pressed well with your silicone spatula.
4. In a separate small bowl, combine the other half of the water (30 grams) and cornstarch. Fold it into the strained currant mixture and mix well.
5. Transfer the mixture back into the clean pot, place it on medium heat. While constantly mixing, allow the confiture to come to a boil. Reduce the heat to medium-low and continue reducing for a few more minutes while constantly mixing.
6. Remove the pot from the stove. Transfer the confiture into a heatproof bowl. Allow it to come to room temperature, then cover it with kitchen plastic/cling film and set it aside.

Assembly:

1. Slice open (horizontally) the cooled cream puffs with a sharp serrated knife. Using a piping bag fitted with a small star piping tip and the peanut butter cream fill/pipe the bottom half of the bun.

2. Add about half a teaspoon of black currant confiture in the center and pipe peanut butter cream over it. Close it with the other half of the cream puff.

3. Pipe a little dollop of cream on top and add a fresh or frozen black currant.

4. Place into the refrigerator for at least an hour to set. Dust with powdered sugar before serving if desired.

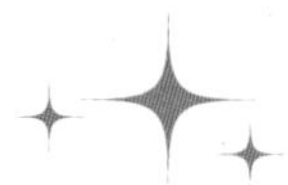

CHOCOLATE MERINGUE TREATS

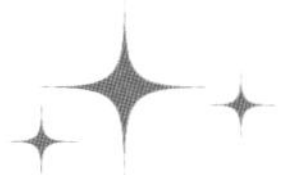

Weighing in grams is essential for the precision and successful result of this recipe. Measurements in cups are not included, nor recommended.

CHOCOLATE MERINGUE:

100 g fresh egg whites, at room temperature

200 g super fine/caster sugar

8 g unsweetened cocoa powder

Chocolate Meringue Directions:

1. *NOTE: Separate your egg whites from the egg yolks while your eggs are cold. Leave the egg whites out to warm up to room temperature for at least an hour.
2. Preheat your oven on the convectional bake setting at 200 degrees Fahrenheit.
3. Prepare a double boiler. Use a pot slightly larger in diameter than the mixing bowl. Fill it with a bit of water and place on medium-high heat.
4. Wipe your mixing bowl and whisk attachment with a bit of lemon juice on a piece of paper towel. Pour your room temperature egg whites and caster sugar into your mixing bowl and place them into a pot with boiling water. Make sure that your mixing bowl with the egg whites and sugar does not touch the boiling water. Reduce the heat to medium-low to ensure that the water is barely simmering.
5. Whisk your egg whites/sugar mixture with your whisk nonstop for 2.5-3 minutes. I use the whisk mixer attachment—fewer steps, fewer dishes to wash.
6. Transfer your mixing bowl onto the mixer and start mixing on low speed for 30 seconds, gradually increasing the speed to medium. Stop the mixer and add the cocoa powder, then start the mixer on low speed again and slowly increase to high. Mix on high speed for 8 minutes. You are looking for stiff meringue here, meaning—when 8 minutes have passed, pull your whisk out and check the meringue's peak—it should just slightly curve.
7. Place the meringue into your piping bag fitted with a Wilton's 8B piping tip and pipe the "Hershey kisses" like dollops, varying in diameter and size if you'd like. I prefer to use silicone baking mats for baking the meringue, but you can use parchment paper if needed. Here is a little tip to prevent your parchment paper from sliding on your baking tray when you pipe meringue—put a little drop or swipe of your meringue onto the baking tray under the parchment paper.
8. Bake for 45-60 minutes on the middle rack. Meringues are ready when you slightly push on them and they do not move. If they are still wiggly, they need to be baked for a few more minutes.
9. Allow your meringue to fully cool off before removing them from your silicone mats or parchment paper. They can be eaten immediately or stored in an airtight container in a dark, dry, cool place for up to a month.

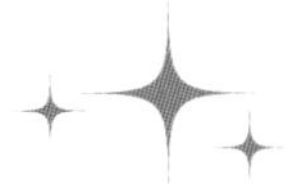

BROWN SUGAR MERINGUE KISSES

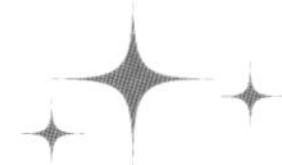

Weighing in grams is essential for the precision and successful result of this recipe. Measurements in cups are not included, nor recommended.

BROWN SUGAR MERINGUE:

100 g fresh egg whites, at room temperature

200 g light brown sugar

Brown Sugar Meringue Directions:

1. Note: Separate your egg whites from the egg yolks while your eggs are cold. Leave the egg whites out to warm up to room temperature for at least an hour.
2. Preheat your oven on the convectional bake setting at 200 degrees Fahrenheit.
3. Prepare double boiler. Use a pot slightly larger in diameter than the mixing bowl. Fill it with a bit of water and place on medium-high heat.
4. Wipe your mixing bowl and whisk attachment with some lemon juice on a piece of paper towel. Pour your room temperature egg whites and light brown sugar into your mixing bowl and place it into the pot with boiling water. Make sure your mixing bowl with egg whites and sugar do not touch the boiling water. Reduce the heat to medium-low to ensure that the water is barely simmering.
5. Whisk your egg whites/sugar mixture with your whisk nonstop for 2.5-3 minutes. I use the mixer attachment whisk—fewer steps, fewer dishes to wash.
6. Transfer your mixing bowl onto the mixer and start mixing on low speed for 30 seconds, gradually increasing the speed to high. Mix on high speed for 8 minutes. You are looking for stiff meringue here, meaning when 8 minutes pass, pull your whisk out and check the meringue's peak—it should just slightly curve.
7. Place the meringue into your piping bag fitted with a Wilton's 1A or 2A piping tip and pipe the "Hershey kisses" like dollops, varying in diameter and size if you'd like. I prefer to use silicone baking mats for baking the meringue, but you can use parchment paper if needed. Here is a little tip to prevent your parchment paper from sliding on your baking tray when you pipe meringue—put a little drop or swipe of your meringue onto the baking tray under the parchment paper.
8. Bake for 45-60 minutes on the middle rack. Meringues are ready when you slightly push on them and they do not move. If they are still wiggly, moving—they need to be baked for a few more minutes.
9. Allow your meringue to fully cool off before removing them from your silicone mats or parchment paper. They can be eaten immediately or stored in an airtight container in dark, dry, cool place for up to a month.

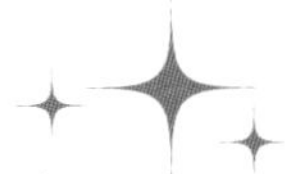

RASPBERRY PISTACHIO MINI TART

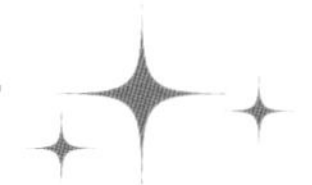

Weighing in grams is essential for the precision and successful result of this recipe. Measurements in cups are not included, nor recommended. *PRO TIP: For Gluten Free version of this recipe, simply substitute the all-purpose flour with 1:1 Gluten Free flour.

SWEET PASTRY TART SHELLS:

125 g all-purpose flour

30 g almond flour

50 g powdered sugar

75 g unsalted butter, cold and cubed

1 pinch of salt

½ egg, beaten

PISTACHIO GANACHE:

220 g heavy cream, cold

100 g high quality white chocolate

20 g pistachio paste

40 g unsalted butter, at room temperature

RASPBERRY CONFITURE:

250 g fresh or frozen raspberry

50 g granulated sugar

3 g lemon zest

8 g lemon juice

60 g water (divided in half)

15 g cornstarch

GARNISH:

Fresh, frozen, or freeze-dried raspberries

Pistachios

Sweet Pastry Tart Shells Directions:

1. Preheat the oven to 350 degrees Fahrenheit.
2. In the food processor or blender, pulse the flour, almond flour, powdered sugar, salt and butter for a few seconds until combined.
3. Add the egg and continue processing until the dough forms a ball.
4. Remove the dough from the food processor/blender and wrap into kitchen plastic/cling film. Place it into the refrigerator for 30 minutes to set.
5. Once the dough has chilled in the refrigerator, cut it into small pieces to soften a bit, then form a ball again and roll it between two pieces of parchment paper to approximately ¼ inch thickness. Place it into the refrigerator for 30–60 minutes to firm it up.
6. Fill your mini tart pans/molds or rings placed over the silicone or mesh baking mats, with the dough. Carefully and gently even out the dough on the bottom and sides of the pans/molds or tart rings.
7. Use a fork to lightly prick the bottoms.
8. Place the filled pans/rings into the freezer for 15 minutes so that they firm up before you start perfecting the edges. Using a sharp knife and holding it perfectly perpendicular to the tart ring, slice out the excess dough that came out from the sides of the pans/rings.
9. Bake the tarts on the middle rack of the oven for approximately 10–15 minutes until they turn to a golden color.
10. Let them cool completely before removing from the pans/rings.

Whipped Pistachio Ganache Directions:

1. Heat the heavy cream to just about boiling point and pour over the white chocolate. Mix well with the silicone spatula.

2. Add the pistachio paste and whip on low speed with a hand mixer or an emerging blender. Allow it to cool to room temperature.

3. Add the butter and whip again. Cover it with kitchen plastic/cling film fully touching the surface of ganache. Place it into the refrigerator for at least 8 hours.

4. Once the ganache sets in the refrigerator, whip it again with the hand mixer or emerging blender, for about 1 minute. Make sure not to overmix.

Raspberry Confiture Directions:

1. Place the raspberries, sugar, lemon zest, lemon juice, and 30 grams of water into a medium sized pot and bring it to a boil on medium heat, constantly mixing with a silicone spatula.

2. Once boiling, reduce the heat to medium-low and allow it to cook for 10–15 minutes.

3. Remove the pot from the stove and immediately strain the confiture into a separate heatproof bowl, making sure all the raspberries are pressed well with your silicone spatula. You should not have more than a few tablespoons of raspberry seeds left in the strainer.

4. In a separate small bowl, combine the other half of the water (30 grams) and the cornstarch. Fold it into the strained raspberry mixture and mix well.

5. Transfer the mixture back into the clean pot and place it on medium heat. While constantly mixing, allow the confiture to come to a boil. Reduce the heat to medium-low and continue reducing for a few more minutes while constantly mixing.

6. Remove the pot from the stove, transfer the confiture into a heatproof bowl and allow it to come to room temperature before using.

Assembly:

1. Fill the cooled tart shells with raspberry confiture and refrigerate for one to two hours to set.

2. Once the raspberry confiture has set and chilled, fit the piping bag with an 8B piping tip and the pistachio ganache. Pipe the dollops of ganache on top of the confiture.

3. Decorate with fresh, frozen, or freeze-dried raspberries and pistachios.

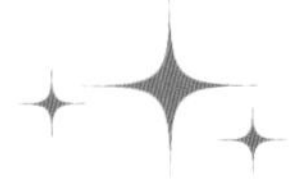

CHOCOLATE BERRY MINI TART

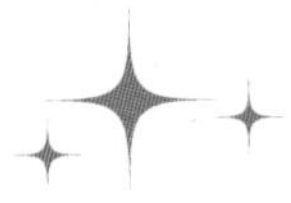

Weighing in grams is essential for the precision and successful result of this recipe. Measurements in cups are not included, nor recommended. *PRO TIP: For Gluten Free version of this recipe, simply substitute the all-purpose flour with 1:1 Gluten Free flour.

CHOCOLATE SWEET PASTRY TART SHELLS:

110 g all-purpose flour

50 g powdered sugar

20 g cocoa powder

25 g almond flour

75 g unsalted butter, cold and cubed

½ egg, at room temperature, beaten

BERRY GANACHE:

10 g blueberry puree, strained

10 g blackberry puree, strained

40 g raspberry puree, strained

55 g heavy cream

125 g high quality white chocolate, chopped

pink or burgundy food coloring gel

GARNISH:

Fresh berries

Edible gold leaf

Chocolate Sweet Pastry Tart Shells Directions:

1. Preheat the oven to 350 degrees Fahrenheit.
2. In the food processor or blender, pulse the flour, almond flour, powdered sugar, cocoa powder and butter for a few seconds until combined.
3. Add the egg and continue processing until the dough forms a ball.
4. Remove the dough from the food processor/ blender and wrap into kitchen plastic/cling film. Place it into the refrigerator for 30 minutes to set.
5. Once the dough has chilled in the refrigerator, cut it into small pieces to soften a bit, then form a ball again and roll it between two pieces of parchment paper to approximately ¼ inch thickness. Place it into the refrigerator for 30–60 minutes to firm up.
6. Drape your mini tart pans/molds or rings placed over the silicone or mesh baking mats, with the dough. Carefully and gently even out the dough on the bottom and sides of the pans/molds or tart rings, making sure not to stretch the dough too much otherwise it will shrink during the baking.
7. Use a fork to lightly prick the bottoms.
8. Place the filled pans/rings into the freezer for 15 minutes so they firm up before you start perfecting the edges. Using a sharp knife and holding it perfectly perpendicular to the tart ring, slice out the excess dough that came out from the sides of the pans/rings.
9. Bake the tarts on middle rack of the oven for approximately 10–15 minutes until crispy.
10. Let them cool completely before removing from the pans/rings.

Berry Ganache Directions:

1. Combine all three berry purees and heavy cream in the medium sized pot and bring to a boil.
2. Pour over the chopped white chocolate and let it stand for 1 minute. Add 3–5 drops of pink or burgundy food coloring gel and mix well with a silicone spatula until all the ingredients have combined to a uniform, smooth finish.
3. Cover it with plastic wrap/cling film – the plastic wrap must be touching and fully covering the surface of the ganache. Set it aside to cool down to room temperature.

Assembly:

1. Pour the chilled berry ganache into the chocolate tart shells. Place into the refrigerator for one to two hours to set.
2. Decorate with fresh berries and edible gold leaf.

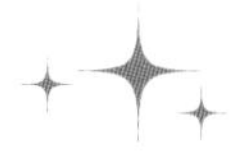

CONVERSION CHART

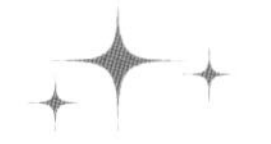

Volume		Weight		Temperature	
U.S.	**Metric**	**U.S.**	**Metric**	**°F**	**°C**
1 tsp.	5 mL	½ oz.	15 g	250	120
1 Tbsp.	15 mL	1 oz.	30 g	300	150
¼ cup	60 mL	3 oz.	90 g	325	160
⅓ cup	80 mL	4 oz.	115 g	350	180
½ cup	125 mL	8 oz.	225 g	375	190
⅔ cup	160 mL	12 oz.	350 g	400	200
¾ cup	180 mL	1 lb.	450 g	425	220
1 cup	250 mL	2¼ lb.	1 kg	450	230

INDEX

R

S

T

U

W

ABOUT THE AUTHOR

A self-taught baker and confectionery artist, Sasha Nary is the creative spirit at the heart of @SashaCakesChicago on TikTok and Instagram as well as a rapidly growing online baking and decorating academy. With her unique blend of classic and contemporary techniques, Sasha inspires and trains bakers from all over the world, using her skills as an instructor to offer fun, accessible, and uplifting courses centered on deliciously colourful recipes.

Originally from Ukraine, Sasha relocated to the United States twenty years ago, submerging herself in a new language and culture all while earning a second degree in business management. During this time, she had also been working full time as an account executive and makeup artistry trainer for major cosmetic brands, using her free time to whip up tasty treats for friends and family. With a passion for all things colourful as well as a desire to take her deep love of baking and decorating to the next level, Sasha eventually decided to embark on a more creatively fulfilling career path. After the birth of her third child, she made the life-changing decision to master her favorite French desserts, diving head first into the world of cake baking and decorating.

From baking her first cake at 8 years old alongside her grandmother to turning her passion into a career after having three amazing kids, Sasha is proud to share her knowledge and experience with aspiring and seasoned bakers alike. Sasha currently resides in the suburbs of Chicago IL with her husband and three kids, who are not only a major support system but also a huge inspiration for tons of recipes and designs!